ABOUT THE AUTHOR

Brian Righi graduated from DePaul University in Chicago and has authored numerous books on occult and paranormal topics, including *Ghosts, Apparitions and Poltergeists: An Exploration of the Supernatural through History*. He first began to chronicle the folklore of vampires while hiking through Eastern Europe, where the lure of the creature still holds sway in the minds of some villagers. Today he continues traveling throughout the United States and other destinations, lecturing on his experiences and investigating claims of the supernatural. He currently calls Texas his home, where he lives with his beautiful wife, Angela; their baby daughter, Sarah; and two lively cocker spaniels, Madison and Dexter. Please visit his website, www.brianrighi.net/.

BRIAN RIGHI

Lore & Legends
of the World's
Most Notorious
Blood Drinkers

VAMPIRES
THROUGH THE AGES

Llewellyn Publications
Woodbury, Minnesota

First Edition
First Printing, 2012

Cover illustration © Victoria Vebell/The July Group
Cover design by Kevin R. Brown

Llewellyn Publications is a registered trademark of Llewellyn Worldwide Ltd.

Library of Congress Cataloging-in-Publication Data
Righi, Brian, 1972–
  Vampires through the ages : lore & legends of the world's most notorious blood drinkers / Brian Righi. — 1st ed.
      p.   cm.
  Includes bibliographical references.
  ISBN 978-0-7387-2648-9
  1. Vampires. 2. Vampires—History. I. Title.
  GR830.V3.R54 2012
  398.21—dc23
                            2011031201

Llewellyn Worldwide Ltd. does not participate in, endorse, or have any authority or responsibility concerning private business transactions between our authors and the public.

All mail addressed to the author is forwarded, but the publisher cannot, unless specifically instructed by the author, give out an address or phone number.

Any Internet references contained in this work are current at publication time, but the publisher cannot guarantee that a specific location will continue to be maintained. Please refer to the publisher's website for links to authors' websites and other sources.

Cover model(s) used for illustrative purposes only and may not endorse or represent the book's subject.

Llewellyn Publications
A Division of Llewellyn Worldwide Ltd.
2143 Wooddale Drive
Woodbury, MN 55125-2989
www.llewellyn.com

Printed in the United States of America

OTHER BOOKS BY THIS AUTHOR

To the "Gentleman of Horror" himself, Peter Cushing, who taught us that all you need in life is to keep your crucifix handy, your stakes well sharpened, and your flask full of good French brandy.

C⊕N✝EN✝S

ACKNOWLEDGMENTS

Writing a book like *Vampires Through the Ages: Lore & Legends of the World's Most Notorious Blood Drinkers* is a lot like raising the dead. It takes a little bit of supernatural mumbo jumbo and a whole lot of hard work. You have to dig deep into the rocky soil of the past on a spooky, moonlit night, among the graves of those who came before you, in order to uncover the secrets buried there over the ages. A piece from here, a nasty bit from there, and a little stitching, and eventually you've created a monster to let loose on the world of mere mortals.

So to all the gravediggers morbid enough to lend their shovel to the work, I would like to take a moment and thank you. To my beautiful wife, Angela, whose patience and support made this possible. To Bill Krause and Amy Glaser at Llewellyn Worldwide, for their hard work and dedication to producing yet another quality book. To all the churchmen, philosophers, writers, and Gypsies who hunted the creatures and added their own tales to the rich tapestry of folklore. Finally, to all those "children of the night" who still roam our modern cities and nightclubs, keeping the dark legends alive.

Introduction:
ONCE BITTEN

I remember well my first frightening encounter with the undead creature that is the subject of this book. I could have been no more than seven or eight years old when it first entered our living room one Friday evening during the late-night creature feature film on television. Though my hands were pressed tightly over my eyes in sheer terror, I could still see enough through the slits of my fingers to take in the frightening scene before me. It was a dark and eerie castle standing high in the mountains of Transylvania. Poor, unsuspecting Renfield had just arrived and entered the dilapidated grand hall, which seemed empty of all but spiderwebs and a creepy soundtrack. Then, from the top of a massive stone staircase, a lone figure appeared, bearing a single candle that struggled against the darkness.

Renfield stopped nervously in his tracks as the figure descended towards him one step at a time. Suddenly the music rose to a dramatic crescendo, and the camera panned in on the figure as it halted on a small landing above. The feeble light cast by the candle revealed the pallid skin and slicked-back hair of Bela Lugosi dressed in a tuxedo and cape. The music died as a devilish smile crossed his face, and in a thick Hungarian accent he exclaimed, "I am … Dracula."

Of course, even by that age the image of the vampire was nothing new to me. I saw his cartoonish face each morning on my box of Count Chocula cereal and in television commercials for everything from toothpaste to used cars, during which he was always taking "a bite out of prices." At one point the count even helped me practice my numbers, as we counted puppet bats together on the children's television program *Sesame Street*, singing out, "ONE, TWO, THREE, AH AH AH AH AH!"

Universal Pictures' 1931 film version of *Dracula*, however, changed all of that for me. He was no longer a comic character with a bad accent, but a horrid figure who stalked unsuspecting prey in order to drink their blood, or who lurked about the closets of small children who watched too many horror movies. Needless to say, I was instantly sold, and from that point on a lifelong fascination with the creature developed. It was no surprise, then, that as each Halloween rolled around I donned my best pair of plastic fangs, and with a cape my mother sewed for me and a distinctive widow's peak penciled onto my forehead, I grabbed my trick-or-treating bag and headed out into the night as Count Dracula. Only, unlike the real vampire portrayed in the movies, I was in search of tasty morsels rather than tasty mortals.

As I grew older, of course, I began to focus on more serious topics, like girls, and the allure of the vampire began to slowly fade along with my childhood. Then one day shortly after college I was confronted by the creature once again in a new and even more startling way, which for the second time in my life transformed my thinking on the topic and inspired my later search for the true origins of the vampire and the writing of this book.

I was traveling through the southern Carpathian Mountains of Romania in the summer of 2001 with a small group of hikers backpacking through Eastern Europe, and after a long day of trekking we wearily stumbled into the village of Zarnesti. Zarnesti is situated at the foothills of the Piatra Craiului National Park, inside the elbow of the mountain range. It is a wild place of deep limestone gorges and dark forests filled with beech and spruce—the hunting grounds of wolf packs and solitary brown bears. After a hearty meal of stuffed cabbage rolls, sauerkraut, and *mamaliga* (a type of cornmeal mush), we lolled back in our chairs as the sun went down, drinking Ursus, a Romanian beer, and watching the locals trickle in. As foreigners, we immediately attracted attention, and as the night grew on more and more villagers approached our table to hear us talk about life beyond the snow-topped wall of the Carpathians. The beer flowed and the villagers sang their lively folk songs describing what life was once like under Communist rule.

As the night wore on, one of my companions eventually asked if there were any vampires about, laughing at his own question as if to dispel the childishness of it. I guess I expected the villagers to laugh also and exclaim how silly we tourists were with our foolish notions, but instead the table grew quiet as if a heavy weight had settled on its drinkers. One old villager, a sheep herder named Alexandru, who drank more than I thought any one person ever could, suddenly turned serious and, in an expressive mix of Daco-Romanian and broken English, began a most curious tale.

According to Alexandru, in the time of his father's father there was a woman who had become a vampire and was terrorizing the village livestock with a wasting disease. In response to the attacks, the local populace dug up her corpse, decapitated it, and drove metal spikes into the body before reburying it. The gruesome action seemed to work, and the curse of the vampire was lifted from the village. During the tale there were many grunts and nods of agreement from other locals positioned around the table, yet by the end of the story not a sound could be heard in the inn save the crackling of the fireplace behind us. It was obvious that this was no mere tale the villagers devised to scare passing tourists. One look in their eyes and it was plain enough to see that they truly believed the old shepherd's account of the facts.

The next day, as we entered the Zarnesti gorge, pushing deeper into the mountains, my thoughts were still occupied with the conversation of the night before. Although it seemed preposterous in this day and age that there were still those who believed the dead could rise from the grave and bring harm to the living, questions began tugging at my mind. Have vampires ever really existed, and if so, how were eyewitness accounts through history different from the pop-culture brand of blood drinker I was raised on?

Certainly the vampire Alexandru described was far removed from the tuxedo-and-cape-wearing creature I was used to, but where did the facts end and the fiction take over? Of even greater consequence, do vampires still exist today? Discovering the answers, I later found, turned out to be a more daunting task than climbing the Carpathian Mountains themselves. It became a hunt that weaved its way through the modern gothic nightclubs of American cities, the desolate burial grounds of Eastern Europe, and dusty library shelves filled with ancient books, on a trail that stretched its way back to the dawn of mankind itself.

Vampires Through the Ages: Lore & Legends of the World's Most Notorious Blood Drinkers chronicles the story of this deadly creature, shedding light on the legends and beliefs, both ancient and modern, that surround it. It will delve deep into humanity's primordial fears of death and damnation, and track down the infamous, real-life blood drinkers of the past and the present whose own bloodlust has added to the gruesome framework of the vampire's tale.

In the process, the book promises to have something for everyone—from the serious scholar in search of the truth, to those living today what we call the modern "vampyre lifestyle," to anyone just wanting to sink their teeth into a good old-fashioned scary story.

So, for those about to undertake this harrowing journey: remember the words in the dedication of this book, and keep your crucifix close and your stakes well sharpened, but above all else—enjoy the hunt.

Throughout the vast shadowy world of ghosts and demons there is no figure so terrible, no figure so dreaded and abhorred, yet dight with fearful fascination, as the vampire ...

—MONTAGUE SUMMERS, *THE VAMPIRE IN LORE AND LEGEND*

1

FROM THE CRADLE TO THE GRAVE

Detectives and mystery writers the world over will tell you that every good story begins with a dead body, but in our case it's the lack of one that sets the stage and introduces the singularly dark mystery that begins our hunt for the truth about vampires. On a cold, dank night in 1933, the murky water of Lake Snagov lapped at a tiny, tree-lined island sitting at its center, with three white towers rising from the concealing foliage of the island's interior—each topped with the distinctive metal cross of the Eastern Orthodox Church. Accessible only by rowboat from a distant cluster of thatched cottages, the Byzantine chapel dominating the island sat like a fortress citadel marking the site of Snagov

Monastery, home to what legend claimed was the final resting place of the Wallachian prince himself, Vlad Dracula Tepes, or as he is better known in the West, Count Dracula.

Already the sun was retreating over the ancient oak forests and marshlands that surrounded the lake and gave this region of Romania a notably wild, almost forbidding reputation. Inside the chapel the shadows lengthened quickly, giving the frescoes of its long dead patrons and saints a more sinister appearance. The votive candles filling the walls and niches did little against the coming darkness and only added to the heaviness of the air with their smoky tapers. Dinu Rosetti and George Florescu flipped on their electric lamps in order to provide more light for the task that lay ahead of them. Assigned by the Romanian Commission on Historic Monuments to excavate the monastery grounds, the two men now stood before the chapel's altar, at whose base a large, unmarked burial stone lay waiting.

Founded in the fourteenth century by the ruler Mircea the Old, the monastery served as more than just a sanctuary for black-robed monks seeking prayer and meditation; over time it was usurped by various rulers as a place for the interment, torture, and execution of their rivals. As the centuries passed and royal dynasties gave way to nation states and political movements, the island became home to condemned criminals and political prisoners, many of whom would never leave the island alive again. During the June through October diggings, the team did indeed find evidence of torture and murder after unearthing a large collection of skeletons, many of which showed signs of decapitation and other violence.

Kneeling down, Dinu gently swept the surface of the stone with a fine brush, stirring up centuries of dust and the strong smell of frankincense. Nervousness gripped them as they laid the tips of their pry bars into the seal of the stone, wondering what they would find beneath the heavy slab. Would it contain the rotting bones of the long-dead prince, infamous for the cruelty he showed to both his enemies and his own people; or did it, as some claim, hold something far worse—something supernaturally evil?

The harsh sound of the stone rising from the floor grated against the chamber walls. Night had fallen completely now, and raising their electric torches the two men peered into the grave with superstitious curiosity. What they found within that dark depression beneath the rich Romanian soil, however, would only further the riddle of Dracula's legend. What they found was an empty grave!

Count Dracula has forever become linked in the Western mindset with one of the most notorious creatures in man's collection of "things that go bump in the night." Despite being called by many names in many languages, it's the term *vampire* that most readily comes to mind when conjuring up images of the blood-sucking monster. The lack of a body that night in 1933 begs many questions that we hope to answer in this book. Besides the obvious considerations of where did the body go and was it ever really buried there, we need to ask ourselves: how did a Wallachian tyrant who died roughly six hundred years ago become connected with the legend of the vampire? In addition, what is a vampire and how did such a fearful creation come into being? Of greatest importance, however, is the question that perhaps only you will be able to decide for yourself—have vampires ever existed, and if so, could they even now be waiting in some dark crypt for night to fall so that they might rise again and threaten humanity with their undying thirst for human blood?

In search of these answers, we'll leave behind the dark monastery of Snagov for now and travel east across mountains and seas, through deserts and valleys, to a land now occupied by modern Iraq. For it is here, in the fertile lands that stretch between the Euphrates and Tigris rivers, known as Mesopotamia, that humanity began to emerge into the history books and forge the cradle of civilization, and as we shall see it is also where the tale of the vampire began its dark rise as well.

RISE ⊕F +HE DEⅢ⊕NS

The earliest hint of a belief in vampires comes to us in the form of archeological evidence excavated from the ruins of the once powerful cities that came to dominate the land between the two rivers. Cuneiform tablets from the First Babylonian Dynasty of the eighteenth century BCE, and depictions on excavated pottery shards revealing scenes of vampires drinking the blood of men, point to a deeply rooted fear among early people of a number of blood-drinking spirits and demons. The Babylonians, for instance, developed a complex hierarchy of demons and other entities stemming from earlier Sumerian origin. Among them there were two general categories that came to be feared above all others.

The first was the dreaded *ekimmu*: evil spirits that had once been human, but could find no rest in the grave. These were some of the most well-documented spirits in ancient Babylon, and their name when translated means "that which is snatched away." Belief held that these spirits were created when a person died a violent and premature death, had left important tasks unfinished, died too young to have tasted love, or most importantly was not buried properly. This included those who had died alone in the desert or had no one left to conduct the proper burial ceremonies and leave food offerings at their tombs. If no offerings were left for the spirits, they would become hungry and leave the underworld to seek nourishment from the living. As Reginald Thompson writes in his book *The Devils and Evil Spirits of Babylonia*, the Babylonians were very clear on what awaited the victims of the ekimmu, believing that "if it found a luckless man who had wandered far from his fellows into haunted places, it fastened upon him, plaguing and tormenting him until such time as a priest should drive it away with exorcisms" (Thompson 1903, xxviii).

These evil spirits often proved the most persistent and difficult to dislodge once they latched onto their victim, and inviting an attack by one could result from actions as simple as gazing upon an impure corpse or touching food contaminated by the spirit. Being a creature of the wind and the darkness, it could also pass through solid objects at will, such as doors or walls. In cases in which the ekimmu resulted from improper burial, performing the appropriate rites was often enough to put the spirit to rest. In other instances, the spirit could be destroyed with weapons made of wood—a defense that would resurface in later vampire traditions in the form of a wooden stake. When all else failed, however, temple priests performed lengthy and elaborate exorcisms, some of which still exist today, as in the form of the following incantation:

The gods which seize (upon man)
Have come forth from the grave;
The evil wind-gusts
Have come forth from the grave.

To demand the payment of rites and the
pouring out of libations,
They have come forth from the grave;
All that is evil in their hosts, like a whirlwind
Hath come forth from the grave.

The evil spirit, the evil demon, the evil devil,
From the earth hath come forth;
From the underworld unto the land they
Have come forth;
In heaven they are unknown,
On earth they are not understood.
They neither stand nor sit
Nor eat nor drink. (Thompson 1908, 7)

A second type of fiendish blood drinker, thought to roam the desert places and city streets alike, was a creature that never existed in human form, but was born of pure evil. Primitive records from the reign of the Babylonians tell of a particularly bloodthirsty demoness referred to as *Lamashtu*, who appears to have evolved from a demoness of even older origin named *Lamme*. As a feared night stalker, Lamashtu ran the gambit of evil doings, including seducing men, harming pregnant women, destroying crops, causing disease, and drinking the blood of the living. In Babylonian theology, she was the daughter of the sky god Anu, who ruled all other gods, spirits, and demons. During the birth of a child, La-mashtu was said to slip into the birthing chamber and feed on the flesh and blood of the newborn, and many a stillborn child's death was blamed on her presence. The only protection afforded to a vulnerable mother and child was through the use of magical amulets and prayers chanted by temple priests during the birth.

Lone travelers were also at particular risk of encountering Lamashtu and were often warned that she made her home in desolate mountains and lonely marshlands. Although, in truth, demons were thought to be formless entities of pure evil, they were often depicted physically with allegorical descriptions that matched their characteristics and traits. Lamashtu, for example, was frequently described as a winged woman with a hairy body and the head of a ferocious lion, or in some illustrations as a woman holding a double-headed serpent in each hand while suckling a dog on her right breast and a pig on her left.

A demonic spirit similar to the Lamashtu was the *gallu*, and though there is some confusion as to whether this was a single entity or an entire class of demons, it was often referred to as part of the "Seven Demons," which took the shape of a raging bull and flew about the cities at night eating the flesh of humans and drinking their blood. These loathsome creatures haunted dark places and were tasked with hauling off unfortunate souls to the underworld. Slaughtering a lamb upon the temple altar or other blood offerings were the only known way to appease them. When such measures failed, the people often turned to their priests, who, as in other cases of demon attack, relied on the power of exorcisms, a fragment of which survives:

Spirits that minish heaven and earth,
That minish the land,
Spirits that minish the land,
Of giant strength,
Of giant strength and giant tread,
Demons (like) raging bulls, great ghosts,
Ghosts that break through all houses,
Demons that have no shame,
Seven are they!
Knowing no care,
They grind the land like corn;
Knowing no mercy,
They rage against mankind:
They spill their blood like rain,
Devouring their flesh (and) sucking
Their veins.
Where the images of the gods are,
There they quake
In the temple of Nabu, who fertiliseth
The shoots of wheat.
They are demons full of violence
Ceaselessly devouring blood.
Invoke the ban against them,
That they no more return to this
Neighborhood.
By heaven be ye exorcised! By earth be
Ye exorcised! (Thompson 1903, 69–71)

Of all the known demons to claw their way out of the walled cities and incense-filled temples of Mesopotamia, one found its most enduring legacy not with the powerful Babylonians, but with a small group of captives from a far-off land known as the Kingdom of Judah. In the Jewish mythology, no demon held such aversion and dismay as that of a winged night demoness named Lilith, who terrified expectant mothers and slumbering men like no other. Some scholars traced the adoption of Lilith to a period of Jewish history known as the Babylonian Captivity, in which Jerusalem was sacked by Nebuchadnezzar II in 586 BCE and its people deported to Babylon. After Babylon was in turn conquered by the Persian Empire in 538 BCE, the Persian ruler Cyrus the Great gave the Jews permission to return to their native land. Although some remained, many returned and brought back with them the traditions and superstitions of their former captors, including a fear of the demoness Lilith.

Much like the Lamashtu from which she originated, Lilith was primarily seen as an infant killer. As a protective measure, many Hebrews wrote in the four corners of their birthing chambers the words "Adam, Eve, begone hence Lilith," or hung special amulets over their child's cradle, which included the names of angels written upon them to act as wards. Also, like earlier incarnations, the Lilith that followed the Hebrews home was a voracious succubus who seduced men in their sleep to obtain their seed in the hopes of spawning demonic offspring of her own. Men waking from fitful dreams to find they had experienced a nocturnal emission were required to recite a prayer the next morning to prevent such an occurrence.

Like many stories passed down over the ages, Lilith's tale is one that transforms with leaps and bounds as each successive culture adopted it as their own. The first mention of a creature called a *lilith* can be found in the Sumerian story of

Inanna and the Hullupu Tree, first set down on clay tablets during the seventh century BCE. In this creation myth, the earth and the sky had just separated from one another when a violent storm arose and uprooted a beautiful willow tree, which rested upon the banks of the Euphrates River. Inanna, the Sumerian goddess of love and war, rescued the tree and planted it among her sacred groves in the city of Uruk. While she waited for the tree to grow large enough to make into a chair and bed for herself, three evil creatures settled on it. The first was a magical snake that coiled itself between the roots; the second was a *lilith*, who made its home inside the trunk; and the third was an anzu bird (a mythological creature much like a sphinx), which nested in the branches. Unable to rid her precious willow tree of these intruders, Inanna turned to her brother Utu, the sun god, but he refused to help. In the end, Gilgamesh, Uruk's famed warrior king, took up the challenge; and after the heavily armed hero killed the snake, the lilith and anzu bird fled in terror.

Such early manifestations suggest that Lilith was initially seen as a vague sort of female spirit, and that it wasn't until she merged with the tales of the Lamashtu that she took on more vampiric qualities. Even then she wasn't viewed as the singular figure we see later on, but rather as a class of *liltu* that were minor owl spirits that attacked humans. As the legend grew, so too did the evils she was said to commit, including being the bearer of storms and disease. Yet it wouldn't be until the Middle Ages that she emerged in the role she became best known for when she began appearing in the rabbinic traditions of the eighth and tenth centuries, most notably in an anonymous medieval text known as the *Alphabet of Ben Sira*.

In this work the author writes that Lilith was the first wife of Adam, but after refusing to take on a subservient role she runs off. When God hears of her rebellion, he becomes angry and sends three angels in pursuit who eventually catch up to her while she is escaping across the Red Sea. Yet despite all their threats, Lilith still refuses to return and submit to Adam. In the end, the angels consent to let her live, but with the warning that each day God would destroy one hundred of her offspring as punishment for her defiance, and from that moment on in the mind of medieval scholars and rabbis, the war between Lilith and man had begun.

As the mythology and superstitions of the Jews interacted and influenced other cultures with which they came in contact, the legend of Lilith underwent an additional series of changes. For instance, in Christian lands during the Middle Ages, Lilith was the wife of Asmodeus, king of the demons, the nine hells, and who represented the sin of lust to the church. The pairing of these two monsters seemed inevitable, and as their story grew the two were said to live in a separate world where they continually created demonic offspring to plague humanity. Many unexplained disasters and calamities were blamed on them, including everything from making men impotent to turning wine sour.

It is also during this period that Lilith takes on her most seductive qualities and was said to always travel with cohorts of succubi to do her bidding. Although Lilith came to be blamed for everything Western patriarchal structures feared the most, including the power of seduction, procreation, and the displacement of gender roles, something far deeper resided in her legends. What revolted the early Hebrews the most was that

Lilith was a blood drinker, and for the tribes of Israel no taboo was greater in the eyes of God than to consume the blood of another.

SAVAGE GODS FROM THE EAST

Even though it might be easy to jump to the conclusion that the precursor to the modern vampire resulted solely from the lands of Mesopotamia, evidence in fact points to the theory that it developed simultaneously from several early sources. While the ancient priests of Babylon were busy exorcising the night demons that plagued their cities, far to the east, in the mist-filled valleys of the Indus River, which borders the western portion of the Indian subcontinent, men were bowing before the blood-drenched altars of strange and fearsome gods. Little is known of the blood cults that originated from the region other than the dark gods they worshiped appeared to demand more than mere obedience; they also wanted human blood.

Wall paintings and carved figures dating back to 3000 BCE have been discovered depicting blood gods with green faces; pale blue bodies; and large, bloodstained fangs. One of the earliest works includes a painting of the Nepalese Lord of Death, who appears standing atop a pile of human bones with massive fangs and a cup of blood shaped from a human skull. Later religious texts would also come to incorporate a belief in blood gods within their pages, including one of the most famous: the *Bardo Thodol*, or *Tibetan Book of the Dead*. Not only does this funerary text describe the passage of the soul after death through the nether regions to rebirth, it also lists as many as fifty-eight wrathful deities known for their blood-drinking appetites.

As worship of the blood gods flourished throughout the river valleys, they eventually spread north to the mountain passes of Tibet and south into the steamy jungles of India, where both the number of blood gods and their power over men grew to new heights. One of the more horrid incarnations to take hold was the Hindu goddess of death and destruction known as Kali, who in many ways came to closely epitomize the image of the female vampire more than any other. Like many of her godly contemporaries, Kali was a spectacle straight from man's darkest nightmares with sharp, bloodstained fangs, a garland of human skulls, and four arms—each bearing a sword or cleaver. Her temples were often located on cremation grounds throughout India, and stories of her taste for blood state that it was so great she once slit her own throat in order to drink the blood that poured from it. Her most memorable tale centers around a battle between herself and the goddess Durga on one side and an unbeatable demon named Raktabija on the other. What made the demon such a dangerous foe was that each time his blood spilled upon the ground he rejuvenated himself. All day long the three battled, with neither Kali nor Durga able to beat the demon. Finally, in a flash of inspiration, Kali gained the upper hand by springing upon the demon and drinking all of his blood. Without his ability to refresh himself, the demon was quickly subdued.

Not only was the goddess Kali responsible for numerous tales of violence and bloodlust, but also for one of the most infamous blood cults the world has ever seen. Beginning sometime in the seventeenth century and continuing into the nineteenth century, a group emerged from the shadows known as the Thuggees, from which we get the English word *thug*. This band of assassins was accused of murdering tens of thousands in the name of Kali before being stamped out by the British in the 1830s. Although many of their practices remain a mystery today, their name continues to live on in legends and through movies like *Indiana Jones and the Temple of Doom*, where they appear as bloodthirsty bad guys.

Members of the clandestine cult are said to have operated in groups posing as common travelers who joined merchant caravans as they passed through remote areas between towns and cities. Once the caravan came to a halt for the night and all its members were asleep, the thugs silently crept from their bedrolls and strangled everyone in the party. The caravan's goods would be looted and all traces that it ever existed destroyed while the bodies of their victims were drained of blood and roasted on a spit before an idol of Kali. In some stories the thugs even drank the blood in order to obtain special occult powers from it.

In 1822, a former British officer named William Sleeman was appointed by Governor General William Bentinck to investigate claims of caravans disappearing in the wilderness. Over the next ten years, Sleeman's police force uncovered evidence of the thugs and eventually tracked down and captured as many as 3,700 cultists, putting an end to their bloody reign once and for all. Many confessed to their deeds and were hanged, while many more were imprisoned for life. Critics of the British crackdown claim that the thugs only existed in the minds of fearful Hindu peasants and that it was nothing more than a modern-day witch hunt. Others contend that the thugs did indeed exist and may even continue their bloody worship of Kali in remote parts of India today.

Similar beliefs in blood gods existed in other parts of the world as well. Egyptians enlisted into their pantheon of gods a particularly brutal warrior goddess named Sekhmet, whose ferocity and bloodlust were matched by no other. Known by a host of monikers, all gruesome of course, including the Scarlet Lady and the Mistress of Slaughter, Sekhmet was often represented as having the head of a lion and the body of a woman. So great was her thirst for blood that she prowled the fields of battle like a lion, drinking the blood and eating the flesh of those who fell in combat. In one of her most celebrated tales, referred to as *The Revenge of Ra*, the sun god Ra creates Sekhmet to punish his rebellious humans for plotting against him. After setting her loose upon the world, Sekhmet quickly devours most of mankind, but when Ra orders her to stop before there are no subjects left, Sekhmet refuses. Fearing her bloodlust has become too powerful, Ra devises a plan to save what was left of humanity. His first step is to turn the waters of the Nile River red so that, mistaking it for blood, Sekhmet will drink from it. Once she begins drinking greedily from the waters, Ra then changes it into beer, causing Sekhmet to become intoxicated and fall into a deep sleep. When she finally wakes from her drunken slumber, she has entirely forgotten her thirst for blood and mankind is spared from annihilation.

Sekhmet's tale was more than just a bedtime story used by the ancient Egyptians to scare small children, however; it was linked to the natural flood cycles of the Nile River, the lifeblood of the land itself. Each year the Nile is inundated with sand and silt from connecting rivers farther upstream, turning the waters blood red and bringing life-giving nutrients to the farmlands that border its course. To celebrate the event, the Egyptians held a yearly festival in which they drank red-colored alcohol in imitation of Sekhmet. Worship of the violent goddess eventually reached its zenith during the reign of Amenemhat I, from 1991 to 1962 BCE, when followers of Sekhmet attained ruling authority over Egypt, and the center of government shifted from its previous location to the headquarters of the cult in Itjtawy.

MONSTERS OF THE WESTERN WORLD

Even from the far-flung coasts of ancient Greece we find early references, in its literature, to various gods, spirits, and other monsters that fed upon the blood of humans. One such creature was Empusa, the daughter of the goddess Hecate, who took the form of a demonic bronze-footed monster that could change into a beautiful woman and feast upon the blood of young men while they slept. Even more feared were creatures known as *striges*, who like the *lilith* of distant Babylon were winged night creatures that either had the bodies of crows and the heads of women or were women who could change into birds of prey at will. In this guise they flew into homes at night where no barrier or lock could keep them out and fed off the blood of sleeping infants and men. It is also said they were particularly fond of human liver and other various internal organs, which they ate with great relish.

The Roman poet Ovid later proposed a number of theories for their origins, including the idea that the creatures were born naturally to their state, that they were once women cursed by the gods to become these monsters, or that they were witches who took on the form through magic spells. The latter of the three explanations would go on to be used by the Orthodox Church to describe blood-drinking witches in league with the devil, who also came to be called *striges*.

Another vampire-like creature that inhabited the rocky Greek isles were female death spirits called *keres*, which were released upon the world when the first woman, Pandora, opened a jar (later mistranslated as "box") containing all the evils to plague mankind. These were terrifying spirits described as dark women dressed in bloodstained garments with gnashing teeth and long talons that hovered over battlefields and drank the blood of the dying and wounded. In what remains of the Hesiodic poem *The Shield of Hercules*, we get a firsthand look at these evil death spirits:

> ... dusky Fates [keres], gnashing their white fangs, lowering, grim, bloody, and unapproachable, struggled for those who were falling, for they all were longing to drink dark blood. So soon as they caught a man overthrown or falling newly wounded, one of them would clasp her great claws about him, and his soul would go down to Hades to chilly Tartarus. And when they had satisfied their souls with human blood, they would cast that one behind them, and rush back again into the tumult and the fray. (Hesiod 1914, 237–9)

Thousands of these vicious spirits were thought to haunt battlefields, fighting among one another over the bodies of the dying like ghastly scavengers. Some stories even include mention of the Olympian gods themselves standing next to their favorite heroes, beating off these clawing death spirits during important battles.

A final vampire-like creature of the early Greeks is the *lamia*, which makes her appearance in the works of such early writers as Aristophanes and Aristotle. Lamia was said to be the daughter of King Belus of Libya and the secret lover of Zeus, king of the gods and ruler of Mount Olympus. When Hera, Zeus's jealous wife, discovered the affair, she immediately flew into a rage and slew all of Lamia's children. Driven mad with grief, Lamia found she could not directly strike back at Hera, so she chose the next best thing and began her revenge by preying upon the infants of mankind instead. From her sprang a race of female vampires that had the torsos of women and the lower bodies of serpents. These creatures were called *lamiae* and were feared not only as child killers but also for their power to transform into beautiful maidens and seduce young men into their bedchambers, where they slowly drank their blood.

In a famous story told by Philostratus in the *Life of Apollonius*, a young man named Menipus falls in love with an exotic woman he meets traveling on the road one day. After a brief flirtation, she convinces him to return to her house in Corinth where the two young lovers begin an amorous affair. The young man's teacher, Apollonius, however, sees through the disguise of the creature and warns the young pupil that he has been enchanted by a lamia. When Apollonius later confronts the creature, she admits to the deception and brags that each time she lay with him she drank a little more of his blood. The story then ends with the monster vanishing and the young man saved from an awful fate. The tale later inspired the English romantic poet John Keats to write his famous poem "Lamia"—only this time the foolish young man perishes from the creature's feeding.

In examining the stories and practices of other cultures, we find that the precursor of the modern vampire arose not from a single source but rather from several—most notably those of Mesopotamia and the Indus River Valley. As the centuries passed, these beliefs were transmitted to new cultures as populations migrated and interacted with one another. Yet nowhere did the fiend find such fertile ground as when it moved its way across the Balkan Peninsula and settled in the dark forests of Eastern Europe. In most cases it traveled in the back of caravan wagons along the trade routes or on the horses of invading foreigners from the east. When the nomadic Magyars crossed the Carpathian Mountains in the fifth century, they settled in lands that came to make up modern Hungary and Romania—lands that later bore witness to the legends of Count Dracula's reign and eventual reincarnation into the vampire we associate him with today.

But in the long history of humanity's migration patterns, no group was as colorful, mysterious, or as closely linked to the legends of the vampire as the Gypsy clans, who appeared at Europe's doorstep in the tenth century. The name given to these dark-skinned wanderers is derived from the mistake that many early Europeans made in assuming they were Egyptians. Often viewed with suspicion in the lands they traveled through, Gypsies carried with them many superstitions concerning death and the life beyond. One of their most powerful and frightening beliefs was that of vampire spirits similar to the lamia of the Greek isles. Among them it was rumored there even existed a sect known as the Cult of

Bibi, which worshiped a demoness that preyed upon the blood of *gorgio*, or non-Gypsy children. Adherents of the evil Bibi also believed the demoness could infect their enemies with epidemics of cholera, typhoid, and tuberculosis.

Regardless of the actual transmission source, the belief in vampire-like creatures spread throughout Eastern Europe like wildfire, infecting the land and its people for centuries to come. Only this time, as it mingled with superstitious populations that still had one foot in Christianity and the other in the paganism of their fathers, a new vampire emerged upon the stage—one that could not be chased away so easily by priestly exorcisms or nullified by bloody sacrifices. Instead, this new horror would claw its way out of the grave and shamble through the night, looking for the blood of innocents to feed upon.

2

NIGHT OF THE LIVING DEAD

In 1968, when George Romero released his independent, black-and-white zombie film *Night of the Living Dead*, audiences were shocked by the darkly lit images of dead bodies rising from the grave to tear at the flesh of the living. The film, which was produced on a $114,000 budget, featured a group of survivors holed up in a rural Pennsylvania farmhouse fighting off wave after wave of mysteriously reanimated corpses. In the end, all of the main characters died, but the movie went on to gain a life of its own, grossing millions over the years with cinematic re-releases and sequels that continue to this day. Despite the fact that it was initially criticized for its graphic content and terrifying storyline, this low-budget tale of the walking dead opened an entire zombie apocalypse sub-genre that forever changed the way audiences viewed horror films.

In today's world, of course, we have the luxury of turning off the television when things get a little scary, but for the small, isolated towns and villages that sprawled across Eastern Europe during the era of the vampire, the fear of corpses wandering about at night knocking on farmhouse doors in search of fresh victims was all too real. These revenants, or reawakened corpses, cast horrifying images in the minds of not only the superstitious peasantry, but also the learned thinkers and writers of the time as well. In the *Harleian Miscellany* of 1810, John Heinrich Zopfius is said to have commented that "the vampyres, which come out of the graves in the night-time, rush upon people sleeping in their beds, suck out all their blood, and destroy them. They attack men, wo'men, and children, sparing neither age nor sex. The people attacked by them complain of suffocation, and a great interception of spirits; after which, they soon expire. Some of them, being asked, at the point of death, what is the matter with them, say they suffer in the manner just related from people lately dead..." (Malham and Oldys 1808, 233).

Other serious minds, such as the famous French Enlightenment philosopher Voltaire, gave a similar definition of the revenant. In his *Philosophical Dictionary*, Voltaire wrote that revenants were "...corpses, who went out of their graves at night to suck the blood of the living, either at their throats or stomachs, after which they returned to their cemeteries. The persons so sucked waned, grew pale, and fell into consumption; while the sucking corpse grew fat, got rosy, and enjoyed an excellent appetite" (1856, 371).

Yet of all the great writers to take a stab at defining the habits and nature of the vampire, it is perhaps John Scoffern who said it best when he said it the simplest: "The best definition I can give of a vampire is a living mischievous and murderous dead body" (1870, 350).

NAMING THE DAMNED

References in English literature to vampiric revenants, however, appear long before these writers put pen to paper; the first mention of the creatures was in a little-known text on English churches in 1679. Although the term *vampire* still hadn't come into print yet, it did begin to surface in popular language sometime after 1688. It wouldn't emerge on the printed page until almost fifty years later, when it finally materialized in a work entitled *Travels of Three Gentlemen from Venice to Hamburg, Being the Grand Tour of Germany in the Year 1734*, by an anonymous author.

The word *vampire* is thought to have been borrowed from the German word *vampir*, which found its genesis in the Eastern Slavic word *upir*, first written in a 1047 translation of the Book of Psalms. In it, the priest transcribing the work from Glagolitic, the oldest known Slavic alphabet, to the Cyrillic of the First Bulgarian Empire in the ninth century writes his name *Upir Likhyi*, meaning "Wicked or Foul Vampire." Although a distasteful moniker such as this seems strange to us today, it is the remnant of an older pagan practice of replacing personal names with nicknames.

Etymologists tracing the roots of the word have branched into four schools of thought over the years, leading to a great deal of lively debate among scholars and folklorists alike.

The first was proposed by German scholars in the 1700s who believed the word *vampire* came from the Greek verb πίνω, meaning "to drink." Later, in the 1800s, a linguist named Franz Miklosich suggested that the Slavic word *upir* and its synonyms *upior*, *uper*, and *upyr* came from the Northern Turkish word *uber*, which meant "witch." In direct opposition to Miklosich, other linguists such as André Vaillant claimed that the Turkish word *uber* was in fact derived from the Slavic word *upir*.

As if all that weren't confusing enough, the final and most recent theory is that the word *vampire* existed no further back than the German-Hungarian word *vampir*, and its origin is relatively new in the scheme of things.

There were, of course, many other names for these creatures, spoken in many other tongues not directly tied to the English *vampire*. For instance, the words *wukodalak*, *vurkulaka*, and *vrykolaka* were found among the Russians, Albanians, and Greeks, all of which translated roughly to mean "wolf-fairy," demonstrating an early comingling of the archetypes for the vampire and the werewolf. Beyond this, the further one digs back through the pages of history, the more obscure and clouded the names become—until they are lost entirely.

CATEGORIES OF VAMPIRISM

Just as the names for vampires changed to suit the tongue they were spoken in, so too did the nature and habits of the creatures change to fit the cultures that believed in them. Despite the many variations on the theme, for the purposes of our investigation vampires can be broken down into three distinct categories. The first and most common form of vampire was

as feared as it was dreadful to behold. These ghastly night stalkers, which we will call *revenants*, were traditionally the corpses
of the living dead, who roamed the night in search of tasty victims, much as George Romero's zombies did in *Night of the Living Dead*. In some cultures the dead bodies were controlled by
the spirit of the deceased, who after death could find no rest
and so was cursed to rise again, while in others the corpse was
merely a rotting vessel inhabited and spurred on by a demon or
other evil spirit. In most cases, revenants were pictured as if
they had just clawed their way out of the grave still wearing
the death shrouds they were buried in. Reports describe them
as shambling monsters with bloated bodies and ruddy or black-
ened colored flesh, long scraggly hair, and ragged claws with
fresh blood seeping from their mouths and nostrils.

In some areas, the revenant took on other physical traits
that departed somewhat from the usual corpse-like appearance—but were equally horrifying. For instance, in the Sa-
ronic Isles of the Mediterranean, revenants had hunchbacks
and attacked with viscous dagger-like claws. In Bulgaria they
had only one nostril, while high on Mount Pelion in central
Greece they glowed in the dark. Among some of the Slavic
and Germanic Gypsies it was even thought that revenants had
no bones, a belief based on the observation that vampires
often left their bones in the grave when they went hunting.
What may surprise many is that the tradition of vampires
sporting sharpened canine fangs was a literary invention that
surfaced much later.

In most cases, what seemed to motivate the revenant was
an insatiable hunger for blood, which it was believed allowed
the creature to continue in its undead state. Upon first awaking

in its coffin, the revenant began to devour its own body, including the funeral shroud it was buried in. The more of itself the revenant consumed, the more its living family members mysteriously began to grow ill and waste away, causing their deaths. At some point in the meal, the revenant either rises from the grave as an invisible spirit through holes in the ground or physically claws its way through the dirt. Once free from its tomb, it wanders through the night in search of family members and relatives to continue its feeding frenzy. After those closest to it have succumbed to its appetites, it turns its attention to former neighbors or even livestock such as sheep or cattle.

Male vampires in particular were said to have strong sexual cravings and often forced their advances on former wives, girlfriends, and other women. Finally, when it can find no more victims within its vicinity, it slowly climbs its way atop the church belfry at midnight and rings the bells so that all who hear the mournful peal will sicken and die. In this manner, revenants such as the Slovakian *nelapsi* were said to have decimated entire villages.

Although when we think of the revenant draining the blood of its victims the common misconception is to envision those telltale puncture marks on the neck, the truth is that most were believed to drain their victim's blood from the heart, stomach, nose, or from between the eyes. Revenants were also blamed for other mischief, including suffocating their victims, damaging their property, causing crops to wither and fail, or bringing bad luck to a household. Among the German and Polish Kashubians, the *nachzehrer*, or "afterwards devourer," could cause a person's death if its shadow simply fell upon them, while the *mwere*, the vampiric spirits of children who died before being baptized, were thought to cause nightmares. One of the most powerful weapons in the revenant's arsenal was known as the evil eye. Belief held that the mere glance of a revenant could cause people to become ill, cursed, or waste away and die. Even inanimate objects were affected by their gaze, causing bread to turn stale, wine to sour, and tools to grow dull and rusty.

Unlike the night demons that swept up from the east and preyed mostly on pregnant women and newborns, the European revenant seemed fixated on those who were closest to them in life; these usually meant immediate family members or others with similar ties. Although being a relation was often enough to become a victim of the undead, other reasons included not observing the proper burial customs of the deceased or somehow causing their death. In Gypsy folklore, being singled out by a *mullo*, meaning "one who is dead," usually meant the victim kept the deceased's possessions after burial rather than destroying them as was the Gypsy custom.

According to most traditions, revenants could only travel about during the night and had to return to their earthly graves before the cock crowed and the sun rose above the horizon—or else they would risk a sort of forced catatonia and the vengeance of angry peasants. The rare exception to this rule is found among the Russians and Poles, who concluded that revenants could attack victims anytime from noon to midnight. It was also held that the creatures were allowed to work their evil any day of the week barring Saturday, which the church dedicated to the Virgin Mary. On this holy day, even witches dared not hold their depraved Sabbaths and all the devil's minions were excluded from conducting their dark business.

Revenants were also thought to be more active during the months right before the feasts of St. George and St. Andrew, when the darkness of the nights lasted their longest and winter blanketed the land like a sort of death itself. Once set free from their tombs, besides general bloodsucking and other foul deeds, revenants were said to haunt deserted crossroads or churchyards, where they perched atop tombstones, rocking back and forth, shrieking in the night. At other times they congregated in remote forests and ruined castles plotting evil deeds together.

The second type of vampire is distinct to the annals of the blood drinkers in that it is a living vampire. In some societies a person could be born a vampire or become one while they were still alive. Those who willingly chose to become a vampire rather than being born one were usually sorcerers or witches engaged in the dark arts. In Romania one of the more feared living vampires was known as *strigoi vii*, which was a type of hag that had two hearts or souls. While they slept, one of their souls left the body and ranged the countryside, drinking the blood of the humans and livestock they came across or reanimating corpses at crossroads to waylay passersby.

Similar to the strigoi vii is an entity of Slavic origin known as the *mora*, which issued forth from the body of a sleeping girl not properly baptized to cause nightmares, suffocation, and a type of wasting illness that sucked the life force from its victim. If the mora then happened to fall in love with her victim, she drank his blood as well.

In addition, living vampires were said to have the unique power to take the "essence" from an object, which interfered with its normal ability to function properly. Therefore hens ceased to lay eggs or cows to give milk; they could even steal the "taste" from bread or the milk from a nursing mother's breast. Living vampires were also blamed for spreading infectious diseases, such as the cholera epidemics that swept through Ukraine in the 1800s, where people were burned to death by their neighbors after being accused of being living vampires responsible for contagion. Another of the usual suspects to mark the list of living vampires were those who suffered from unexplained trances or sleepwalking. In Greece it was believed that those prone to somnambulist wanderings would be seized by an uncontrollable bloodlust and go forth biting and tearing at every man or beast they came across.

In most cases, the powers or traits of the living vampire were considered hereditary and could be passed from one generation to the next. In certain southern Slavic folklore, this first began with the vampire starting off as an invisible shadow that gained strength as it sucked the lifeblood of the living. It then formed into a jelly-like mass that grew more defined, until at the end of forty days it had shaped itself into a human-like body identical to the one it had while it was alive. These vampires then, usually male, but in some rare stories female as well, traveled to another village where they were unknown to the inhabitants and married, producing offspring. The children in turn became living vampires who not only had the power to see invisible vampires but also to destroy them. Legend states that when these vampires finally died, they returned again to haunt the living as revenants.

The final category of vampire is a catch-all, really, for some of the most obscure and unusual blood-drinking creatures to grace the early folklore of Europe. One of the more colorful such vampires was a murderous dwarf with a Scottish accent found in the border tales that circulated between Scotland and England. Known by the name *redcap*, this red-eyed, long-toothed, bloodthirsty fairy inhabited ruined castles and ambushed unsuspecting travelers. After lopping off their heads with heavy iron pikes, the redcaps dyed their hats in the blood of their victims—hence the name they were known by.

This vile practice was more than a bad fashion statement, however, because if the blood were ever allowed to dry, the redcap would die. Despite wearing iron-shod boots, they were also renowned for their speed, and it was said to be impossible to outrun one. The only defense, therefore, was to recite biblical scripture aloud and make the sign of the cross, which was guaranteed to drive them away. In one popular legend, Lord William de Soulis, a Scottish border noble during the Wars of Scottish Independence, was rumored to have kept such a creature named Robin Redcap as a familiar. Unfortunately for Lord William, this particular redcap could not be contained very long even through the most powerful of dark arts, and it was soon wreaking havoc in the lands surrounding its master's dwelling at Hermitage Castle. Eventually, Lord William was able to wrap the redcap in lead and boil it to death in an ancient circle of stones known as the Nine Stane Rigg. Historically, though, Lord William fared little better and was imprisoned in Dumbarton Castle for conspiring against Robert the Bruce, dying there under cloudy circumstances in 1321.

More fantastic than the redcaps of Scotland were the shapeshifting *alps* of Germany. Said to take the shape of any animal or insect it wished, including butterflies, cats, pigs, birds, or dogs, the alp always wore a magical hat that granted it supernatural powers such as invisibility or the dreaded evil eye. Feared for their ability to cause nightmares, alps were also known to sexually molest both men and women in their sleep and entered their bodies through the mouth in the form of a mist or snake. In some cases, alps also drank the blood of their victims through the nipples and could cause the milk of both nursing mothers and cows to dry up. As frightening as the alp was to the German peasantry, the remedy to combat it was as simple as it was strange: all a person needed to do was to sleep with his or her shoes next to the bed, pointing towards the door.

Often classed with these types of vampires was a breed of European eclipse demon known in Serbia as the *varcolac*, whose demanding appetite was blamed for devouring the sun and moon during an eclipse as well as bringing storms and ruining crops. Recognized by their pale faces and dry skin, they were famous for their capacity to drink boiled milk, wine, and vodka as if it were mere water. Although they could be mistaken for normal humans during daylight hours, at night their spirit left their body while it slept and, taking the form of various animals, hunted the moon and the sun. During an eclipse, nervous villagers often banged pots and pans together or beat loud drums to chase away the varcolac.

In one popular tale a Serbian peasant lost his fortune after one of these fiends destroyed his vineyards with a terrible storm. Determined to seek his revenge, the man vowed to wait under a pear tree with a shotgun loaded with gold, silver, lead, and steel shot for the varcolac to return. Then one day the sky suddenly grew dark and tumultuous, and a varcolac appeared in the shape of an eagle. The peasant took aim, and with a single blast of his shotgun felled the creature, which died as it hit the ground, causing the sky to immediately clear.

Far more astonishing than any of these bloodsucking monstrosities was a belief among some groups that even everyday objects such tools or fruit could become vampires. For instance, in the Balkans if a tool were left outside under a full moon, it could become a vampire and cause its owner much mischief. Wooden knots for a yoke or the rods for binding sheaves of wheat could, if left undone for more than three years, conceivably turn into vampires. According to some Gypsy traditions, watermelons and especially pumpkins if kept for more than ten days after Christmas would start to bleed and roll around on the ground, making alarming noises. Vampire fruit seemed cause for little concern though, as even then everyone knew that fruit had no teeth.

THE ART OF BECOMING A VAMPIRE

Just as there existed a number of variations on the vampire theme in folklore of the period, there were also many ways by which one could be created. One method of explaining their existence rested more on ill fate and bad genes than anything else, and a belief that some people were naturally born to be vampires. The Slavic people of Hannover, Germany (who were also known as *Wends*), for example, thought that if a child returned to its mother's breast after being weaned, it was a *Doppelsauger*, or "double sucker." From then on the child was destined to seek nourishment it could never satisfy, even rising from the grave after death to feed on the living. As with many revenants, its consuming hunger was so great it not only drained the vitality of its living relatives but also devoured its own corpse and burial clothes. Also rumored to become vampires were those born under inauspicious circumstances, such as the seventh son of a seventh son or the illegitimate child of illegitimate parents. Even being born on the wrong day was enough to do the trick in some regions. Christmas Day for one was said to be a bad time to be born, as it meant a person would become a vampire after death as divine punishment for the presumptuousness of his mother in daring to give birth on the same day as the holy Virgin Mary.

Birth defects and other physical oddities that set one apart from the rest of the village also played a part in marking those fated to become such creatures. Early men often viewed physical defects as an expression of some deeper spiritual deficiency or curse. Probably the most common was the presence of the caul at the birth of an infant. The caul is a thin membranous sac that covers the baby's face and body during birth, and if it remained intact it was thought to be an omen that the child would grow to acquire supernatural powers for good or evil. If, unfortunately, the thin, filmy membrane burst and the infant swallowed part of it, he was doomed to become a vampire.

Among the Kashubians of Poland, the caul was saved until the child's seventh birthday, when it was reduced to ashes and fed to the child as an antidote against vampirism. Numerous other traits existed that branded one as a future vampire, including physical deformities such as a hunchback or an unusual birthmark. In Greece, merely having eyebrows that grew too closely together meant you were singled out for the fate.

The second method of becoming a vampire was reserved for those who lived what the early Christian church deemed an evil or unholy life. The offense was applied to anyone, from church heretics and priests who took mass in a "state of sin" to murderers and other criminals. In some regions, simple acts such as stealing the ropes used to lower a coffin into the grave or eating the meat of animals killed by wolves was enough to receive this punishment. The worst offenders, of course, were those who sold their soul to the devil or engaged in the practice of witchcraft. This included living vampires, werewolves, or the offspring of evil unions between witches and devils, all of whom continued on as undead revenants after death. In addition to the curse being a sort of divine retribution for living a life of wickedness, it also meant that the person would not be buried in consecrated ground. Instead of internment in a churchyard, such people suffered the ignoble fate of being buried in secret at lonely crossroads or in unmarked gravesites so that their spirits could not find their way back home. In such a state the corpse became more than just food for the worms, but a corrupted vessel that all manner of evil spirits and demons could possess to meet their own bloodthirsty needs.

The third method revolved around one of early man's misconceptions of sudden or unexplained death. Although the average life expectancy of the Eastern European peasant was much shorter than ours today, unexpected deaths were still a bit of a shock back then. In the thought process of our ancestors, death was an unnatural event that if transpired before its time could leave a spirit wandering aimlessly throughout the land looking for revenge. Being killed by wild animals in the forest, dying alone, drowning, murder, and suicide were all examples of an untimely death. Even passing away on the wrong day could be an accursed event, as in some Southern Slavic countries, where dying between Christmas and the celebration of the Epiphany meant one might return as a vampire. The Wallachians often equated the sudden occurrence of death to an attack by a vampire and took great precautions when burying those who had died mysteriously.

Besides unexplained deaths, another obviously effective way was to die at the hands of a vampire. In most of the literature, including modern fiction, vampirism is a contagion spread by contact between the vampire and its prey. In some reports, even those who survived a vampire attack still ran the risk of becoming one after they died. Coming into contact with the blood of a vampire in some folklore worked as an antidote, while in others it spread the condition like a disease. The Serbs and Croats of Herzegovina believed that when piercing the suspected corpse of a vampire with a stake (which we'll read about in later chapters), it should be done through the dried hide of a young bull to keep the blood from splattering and infecting the vampire killer.

The final method of becoming a vampire was often associated with digressions from local burial customs that marked a lack of respect for the body of the deceased. For example, in the folklore of the Balkans, if a cat or dog jumped over the body while it awaited burial the corpse could come back from the dead as a revenant. Tradition held in many cases that the body should be guarded by a family member whose job was to ensure nothing went wrong with the complex burial customs of the time. An animal being allowed in the room, much less desecrating the body, was a major breach of protocol. Other prohibitions warned against shaking hands over a corpse, letting the shadow of a person fall upon it, or passing an object such as a candle across it. Each of these admonitions carried with it the threat that if proper respect was not shown for the dead, dire consequences awaited the living. A botched burial, after all, meant a glitch in the process by which the spirit successfully left the body for good. Disrupting this ensured the spirit would return and crave the sustenance of human blood.

THE CASE ⊕F PE+ER PL⊕G⊕|⊕WI+Z

Although we have examined the nature and habits of the vampiric creatures that stalked Eastern Europe in the years leading up to the 1800s, it's difficult to grasp the impact of their bloodthirsty activities on local populations without examining actual reports of vampire attacks from the period. By the mid-1700s, a vampire scare was sweeping across the continent from the shores of the Black Sea in the east to the monarchies of Western Europe. Printing presses streamed with pamphlets, and each day newspapers competed with one another over cataloging the grisly details of fresh vampire assaults in the small villages and lonely mountain passes of the far-off Balkans. One of the first well-documented cases of vampirism to still exist was published in a Viennese newspaper, *Wienerisches Diarium*, and concerned a Serbian peasant named Peter Plogojowitz.

In 1718, after a bitter and bloody contest, a treaty known as the Peace of Passarowitz was signed between the Habsburg monarchy of Austria and the ailing Ottoman Empire. Under the agreement, Austria and her allies, the Republic of Venice, were handed parts of Serbia and Wallachia, which had long lay under the Turkish yoke. Suddenly, lands normally isolated from the rest of Europe were swarming with imperial soldiers and bureaucrats sending back dispatches about their new subjects to the recently installed monarchy.

On July 31, 1725, an official report was issued by an Imperial Provisor named Frombald, claiming to have witnessed the disinterment and staking of a corpse suspected of being a vampire. Sometime during the year 1725 a man named Peter Plogojowitz died in the Serbian village of Kisolova, which today can be found just east of Belgrade on a small island on the Danube River and has been renamed Kisiljevo. Ten weeks following his burial, villagers began whispering in frightened tones that his corpse was seen walking through the narrow streets at night. Within the space of eight days, nine people died mysteriously, all of whom claimed upon their deathbed that the figure of Plogojowitz had visited them in their sleep and attacked them. As the stories grew louder, Plogojowitz's former wife spoke out and admitted that he had returned to her one night as well demanding his *opanci*, or shoes. Terrified by the encounter and the growing death toll, she soon packed her belongings and moved to another village.

By now panic gripped the tiny hamlet, and the inhabitants turned to the imperial representative of the district, Provisor Frombald, for permission to exhume the body of Peter Plogojowitz and examine it for signs of vampirism. Initially the Provisor tried to stall, claiming that he first needed to inform the Austrian authorities in Belgrade, but the villagers would not be swayed and threatened to abandon the village if their demands were not met. After all, this was not the first time the village had been exterminated by vampires, which they claimed occurred once before while under Ottoman rule and they were not about to let it happen again. Fearing their growing anger, the stubborn Frombald was forced to consent and with the Gradisk parish priest accompanied the growing crowd of villagers to the town cemetery. To their surprise, once the body was brought to the surface and the burial wrappings torn away, the corpse appeared undecayed with new skin and nails growing under the old and with what resembled fresh blood around the mouth. In his report Frombald also mentions what he delicately termed "wild signs," which out of respect for the reader he refused to elaborate on. Later commentators explained that it alluded to the corpse having an erection, a recurring element that may have later helped associate the vampire with its erotic elements.

Given these and other curious signs, the people grew greatly distressed and drove a stake through the heart of the corpse—immediately sending a fountain of blood spraying upwards, which welled out of the mouth and ears as well. The body was then dragged from the grave and set on fire with torches. The Provisor finishes his story, as any good bureaucrat looking to keep his job would, by stating that although he was opposed to the actions of the villagers, they could not be stopped from the hysteria that swept them and that he should not be blamed.

THE CASE ⊕F ARN⊕D PA⊕LE

A second account to find its way into the headlines of the day occurred in the year 1727 in yet another small Serbian village, this one named Medvegia. According to the story, a man named Arnod Paole settled in the village after many years of military service fighting the Turks. In 1725 he died from a fall off a hay wagon, breaking his neck, and was buried in the local cemetery in the provincial manner. Thirty days after his burial, residents of the village began to report that they were being haunted by his spirit at night. Soon after four of these witnesses died, the village began to clamor that Arnod Paole had returned from the dead as a vampire. Helping to fuel the growing suspicion, it was widely gossiped that while he was alive, Paole related to his wife that he was once attacked by a vampire while serving in the Turkish controlled town of Gossowa (perhaps Kosova). To avoid becoming one of the creatures himself, he exhumed the corpse of the vampire that attacked him and disposed of it in the accustomed manner for dealing with such things. Following the traditional remedy, he also smeared the blood of the corpse on his body and consumed some the grave dirt.

As the nightly attacks by Paole continued, the villagers grew more frightened, not knowing who among them would become his next target. Finally, a *Hadnack*, a type of military administrator, who was well acquainted with the lore of the vampire, suggested to the village elders that the only way to combat the menace threatening their homes was to disinter the body of Arnod Paole and drive a stake through it. Fearing that if they did not act swiftly the entire village would be lost, a group of men nervously raised the body of Paole from the grave. Upon examining the corpse, they were shocked to find it undecayed and that "fresh blood had flowed from his eyes, nose, mouth, and ears; that the shirt, the covering, and the coffin were completely bloody; that the old nails on his hands and feet, along with the skin, had fallen off, and that new ones had grown" (Barber 1988, 160).

Convinced that these strange signs marked Paole as the vampire plaguing their village, the men drove a stake through his heart, immediately causing the corpse to let out a terrible groan and sending a massive amount of blood flying from the wound. The body was then dragged from its coffin, the head cut off, and the remains burned, before being returned to the grave. In like manner the bodies of the victims were also exhumed and treated to prevent the vampirism from spreading.

After this, things seemed to quiet down for a time until the winter of 1731, when as many as ten villagers died in the space of a few weeks from an unknown illness that caused pain in the sides and chest, prolonged fever, jerking limbs, and finally death. Panic consumed the village once more, and there was talk that vampires were yet again at Medvegia's doorstep. The village elders in turn appealed to *Oberstleutnant* Schnezzer, the Austrian military commander of the region, for help. He, however, feared an outbreak of disease rather than of vampires and sent an infectious-disease specialist, one Doctor Glaser, to investigate the reports. Glaser, after examining the villagers and their homes, was nevertheless at a loss to explain the cause of the inexplicable deaths. By now the situation had reached such a pitch that terrified villagers were banding together at night in groups for protection. Glaser's only recourse was to suggest to his superiors that they allow the village to exhume and "kill" the supposed vampires in order to appease the growing delirium.

Taking the good doctor's advice, the Supreme Commander of Belgrade, Botta d'Adorno, elected to send a commission of military officers and surgeons under the direction of Doctor Johann Flückinger to investigate the matter. On January 7th, under the watchful eye of the commission, the elders of Medvegia hired a group of passing Gypsies to open the graves of suspected vampires in the village cemetery and search them for signs of the curse. In all, thirteen of the seventeen corpses exhumed appeared undecayed, with fresh blood around the mouth and what looked to be new skin and nails growing under the old. One corpse, belonging to a sixty-year-old woman who was known for her thinness in life, was found bloated and full of blood. Some of those bearing the marks of the vampire belonged to the same men who helped destroy the corpse of Arnod Paole, and in doing so had smeared their bodies with his blood for protection.

After the surgeons performed their medical examinations of the corpses and agreed that the bodies bore the traditional signs of the vampire, the hired Gypsies cut off the heads, burned the remains, and scattered the ashes into a river. Doctor Flückinger submitted the details of the incident in a report entitled *Visum et Repertum*, or "Seen and Discovered," which he sent to the Imperial Council of War at Vienna. Following this second round of purging, the villagers seemed content in the belief that they were now finally free of the vampire scourge.

Part of the reason these two cases caught the public imagination so powerfully was that they were so well documented and involved official government investigations, lending them an air of credibility. Picked up by a hungry press, they were told and retold across Europe with a speed faster than ever before. Theologians and philosophers debated their existence, and writers cashed in on the stories. The problem worsened even more when credulous peasants, caught up in the fervor, began digging up and desecrating bodies at an alarming rate. Dismayed by the increasing trend, Empress Maria Theresa of Austria ordered her personal physician, Gerhard van Swieten, to investigate the claims of vampires infecting her territories to the east.

In the end, van Swieten concluded that the creatures did not in fact exist outside the superstitious minds of the peasantry, and the empress enacted strict laws prohibiting the further desecration of bodies. Although the belief persisted among local populations (even today there are occasional reports of this occurring in remote eastern areas), this crackdown effectively sounded the end of the vampire panic. Yet despite the new laws and official government denials, the image of the vampire did not diminish, but found new life as its legend continued to grow and change through the centuries, becoming stronger and more feared than ever before.

Be careful when you fight the monsters, lest you become one.
—FRIEDRICH NIETZSCHE

3

IN THE SHADOW
OF THE CROSS

When Christianity first landed on the shores of Italy around 40 CE, the belief in vampires had long existed among the pagan peoples of Europe. Born from the teachings of a small rabble of Jewish missionaries, Christianity spread across the land replacing, incorporating, or conquering all others before it. Initially the fledgling church met with stiff resistance from Roman rulers, who scoffed at its monotheistic doctrine of salvation and were enraged that believers refused to bow before Roman divinity. Almost from the start, persecutions hounded the new faith wherever it cropped up, and accusations of child sacrifice, cannibalism, and blood drinking were commonly leveled against it.

In even the farthest-flung provinces of the Roman Empire, Christians were dragged from their homes and imprisoned or tortured until they denounced their faith. Those who refused faced the threat of public execution in the arena by some of the cruelest methods possible, including crucifixion, burning at the stake, stoning, or within the jaws of a hungry lion. Conditions such as these drove the church underground, and small groups were forced to congregate secretly in the back rooms of homes or in the dark catacombs of the city's burial grounds.

Eventually the storm of Roman persecutions passed, and Christianity came to outlast even the Caesars themselves. What began as a grassroots movement among the downtrodden and displaced in time gained inroads into the more affluent levels of society as well. In 312 CE, Emperor Constantine I adopted the cross as his standard at the Battle of Milvian Bridge after a vision from God guaranteed him victory should his men fight under the Christian symbol. Following this miraculous victory over a much larger force, Constantine converted to Christianity and went on to become the sole ruler of the Roman Empire. Suddenly the church found itself at the head of a vast kingdom stretching from the misty isles of the Britons to the exotic lands of North Africa and the ancient kingdoms of the East.

DARK DAYS

At the beginning of the church's reign, it paid little heed to the issue of vampirism, preferring to view it as the product of backward pagan imaginations to be discouraged with the light of reason whenever possible. In 1054, however, an event occurred that shook Christianity to its very core and ushered in a new age of turmoil and strife that forever changed the face of the church and forced it to confront such beliefs head on. Known by historians as the "Great Schism," the change came about when the Eastern and Greek section of the church centered in Constantinople formally broke from the Western and Latin section based in Rome. The East, with its inclination towards philosophy and mysticism, became known as the Eastern Orthodox Church, while the West, which was guided by a more legalistic mentality, became known as the Roman Catholic Church.

Of course nothing was cordial about the split, as Pope Leo IX of the Roman branch excommunicated the Patriarch of Constantinople, Michael Cerularius, who returned the favor with his own excommunication of the pope. Both sides pointed to doctrinal issues such Rome's claim to universal papal supremacy or changes to the Nicene Creed, but the truth of the matter lay in larger factors that were sweeping the land at the time, affecting not only the church but the very fabric of European society itself.

Europe was entering one of the darkest periods in its history, filled with waves of foreign invaders, internal conflicts, devastating wars, famines, and unstoppable plagues that consigned entire villages to the grave. Weakened by divisions, heresies, and a growing Islamic presence in the east, it's only natural that cracks should appear within the church. How they reacted to these pressures, however, was a different matter altogether, as the church found itself taking an increasingly harder line against anything that threatened its security and supremacy.

As early as 1184, the Roman Catholic branch reacted by sanctioning a series of inquisitions to stamp out heretics and other enemies of the church, which for the first time included

witches and vampires. What was once the superstitious imag-
ining of ignorant pagans was now public enemy number one
in the eyes of the church, and even the most learned churchmen found themselves fearing the impenetrable forests and
lonely crossroads at night, which they supposed teemed with
all manner of vampire and devil. At first the religious tribu-
nals of inquisitors had no more authority than to imprison or
fine offenders, but as their power grew so too did their methods of persuasion, and untold numbers of innocent lives were
lost at the hands of overzealous inquisitors who tortured and
burned in the name of God.

With the church taking a much keener interest in the existence of vampires, it would come to produce some, if not
all, of the most reliable research over the next few hundred
years on the topic. Not only did church scholars, priests, and
monks begin studying vampirism, but they also cast the creatures to fit more accurately within the Christian framework.
In 1645 the Roman Catholic scholar and trained physician
Leo Allatius penned the first systematic approach to vampires, entitled *De Graecorum hodie quorundam opinationibus*,
which when translated means "On Certain Modern Opinions
among the Greeks."

In this groundbreaking work, Allatius turned his attention
to the Greek vampire, or *vrykolakas*, and transformed it from
its previous pagan origins of the walking dead to a more sub-
limely evil creature enlisted to do the work of the devil. In one
of the book's most often-quoted passages, Allatius writes that
"the corpse is entered by a demon which is the source of ruin
to unhappy men. For frequently emerging from the tomb in
the form of that body and roaming about the city and other

inhabited places, especially by night, it betakes itself of any house it fancies, and, after knocking at the door, addresses one of the inmates in a loud tone. If the person answers he is done for: two days after that he dies" (Wright 1987, 38).

One the sources Allatius relied heavily upon as an authority for the work was the dreaded *Malleus Maleficarum*, or *The Witch's Hammer*. Written in Germany in 1486 by the inquisitor Heinrich Kramer, the book was the witch-finder's bible of its time and laid out the system by which witches existed and the procedures to find them out and convict them. Three conditions were said to be necessary for witchcraft to exist, which he noted were the devil, the witch, and the permission of God. Allatius likewise applied the same formula to the vampire, which the *Malleus Maleficarum* called *succubus*, and claimed that for vampires to exist all that was needed was the dead body, the devil, and the permission of God.

ANCIEN+ F⊕ES

To the masses of European peasants who depended on the early church for its knowledge and divine protection against all evil creatures, the holy men who made up the church's ranks were the superheroes of their time. Compared to the damnation and chaos the vampire represented, the church promised salvation and order—a light in a land that seemed to be devoured by darkness. The priest, after all, was the first one you called if you suspected a vampire may be lurking in your neighborhood, for it was he who had the knowledge and authority to fight such monsters. This relationship forever defined the church as the nemesis of the vampire in the traditions that followed, mixing the Christian motifs of crucifixes, holy water, blessed objects, the Eucharist, and sacred ground into the legends of the ancient creature.

For example, in the 1190s the English historian and churchman William of Newburgh drafted a fascinating work entitled *Historia rerum Anglicarum*, or the *History of English Affairs*, in which appeared the tale of a revenant plaguing the countryside. The sinister event was said to have occurred in the vicinity of Melrose Abbey, a monastery in the south of Scotland founded by an order of Cistercian monks in 1136. A priest famous for his corrupt and sinful ways, known as the "Hundeprest" because of his love for hunting rather than performing his religious obligations, died one day and was buried in the abbey's adjacent cemetery. Soon after his demise, his corpse was seen wandering through the cemetery at night. At first the loathsome creature tried to enter the abbey but found it could not cross the holy structure's entrance on account of the prayers of the monks within.

Forced away, the revenant roamed the countryside making terrible noises until it reached the bedchamber of its former mistress. Night after night it appeared to her until she could take no more and appealed to the monastery's friars for help. To answer her desperate pleas, four monks set themselves over the priest's tomb at night armed with whatever weapons they could find. The night was cold, and as midnight approached three of the monks left to warm themselves at a nearby house. No sooner had they passed from view than the revenant appeared to the remaining monk and rushed upon him with a terrible noise. The monk remained firm, however, and struck the creature with a mighty blow from his axe, causing it to retreat once more back into its grave. The next morning, the four monks gathered at the tomb of the priest and found the corpse with a large wound upon its side matching that of the monk's axe from which fresh blood still flowed, filling the grave. The monks then carried the body some distance from the monastery, where they burned it and scattered the ashes to the wind.

A second account from the same source was reported to William of Newburgh by the archdeacon of Buckingham-shire and other religious men whom he does not name. Accordingly, in the county of Buckinghamshire, northwest of London, a certain man died and was laid in a tomb on the eve of Ascension Day, which is celebrated forty days after Easter and marks Christ's ascension to heaven. Unexpectedly, on the following night the deceased man appeared in the bedchamber of his wife and nearly smothered her to death with his weight. For three nights these attacks continued until the wife surrounded herself with companions to guard her sleep, who chased the revenant away with loud shouts and other noises.

Denied one victim, it turned its attention to others in the village, who were also forced to keep guards while they slept. Even the village livestock was not safe from its evil mischief. Eventually the creature became bold enough to appear in day-light and assault its victims even while in the midst of groups of people. After some time of this, the inhabitants of the vil-lage could take no more and turned to the archdeacon of the county for help, who having no experience in such matters wrote to Bishop Hugh of Lincoln for instructions. The bishop, who was later canonized as a saint, consulted various church scholars of the time and was amazed to learn that such crea-tures had plagued other parts of Britain over the years and that the only remedy was to burn the revenant's body. The thought of burning the body seemed sacrilegious to the bishop, however, so he wrote a letter of absolution with his own hand and ordered it placed in the grave of the vampire. When the letter arrived back at the village, the man's tomb was opened and the letter placed upon its chest, and thereafter he never appeared again.

A final tale to help drive the point home can be found in William Ralston's 1872 *Songs of the Russian People*, which despite its name is actually a book featuring some of the greatest examples of Slavic mythology, tradition, and folklore ever written. In one passage there is a brief tale about a terrible sinner who died one day and was taken to the local church so that a vigil could be kept over the body in preparation for burial. The sacristan who was to keep the watch and recite the psalms was a clever man and brought along a rooster with him. That night, as the twelfth hour approached, the corpse sprang from the coffin, and with its deadly jaws opened wide, rushed at the man. The sacristan quickly gave the bird a pinch, causing it to crow at that very moment. Thinking dawn had come, the vampire fell to the ground a motionless corpse.

Tales such as these played a role in the lives of the average European peasant that extended beyond mere storytelling. They also reinforced critical stereotypes the church wished to espouse, the most important of which was that the church could explain the existence of the creatures and knew how to dispose of them. Whether through divine prayer, absolution, the cold steel of an axe, or the cunning of the clergyman, the church was asserting its authority over the vampire. In almost every report or fragment of folklore to be found on vampires, one of the first things the frightened villagers do in each case is to enlist the aid of the local priest.

EXCOMMUNICATION

Even though both branches of the church seemed to develop a deep fascination with vampires and vampirism, the topic without a doubt found its most fertile ground in the domains of the Eastern Orthodox Church where pagan traditions still heavily influenced the people. One important circumstance that helped foster the belief in vampires was the church's doctrine that the fate of a person's soul was inexorably linked to the condition and care of the body after death. In the Eastern Orthodox Church there were generally five prescribed types of funeral rites that could be performed depending on the deceased's station in life, which included services for laymen, children, monks, priests, and a special service for those buried during Bright Week, which is the week of Easter.

As discussed in the preceding chapter, funerary rites were closely observed to ensure the safety of the soul during its passage from the body to the afterlife, and any breach in the ritual could have dire consequences not only for the deceased but for the entire village. The process began with the corpse being ceremonially washed and anointed with sacred oils before being put on display in the home for a period of time. After the wake, the deceased was carried to the church, where services were conducted for the repose of the soul. The body was then placed in an anteroom of the church, where priests kept a vigil throughout the night reciting prayers and reading aloud from the Bible. The next morning a procession of mourners bearing crosses, flags, and censers of frankincense escorted the body to its final resting place, where more services were conducted and the coffin was lowered into the ground to be covered by dirt. Traditionally the church buried its dead facing the east towards the rising of the sun and then oriented the grave marker, which was usually a cross, at their feet rather than their head to ensure that the soul could pray facing the cross while it waited to be freed from the body.

After it lay in the ground for a specific period of time, priests and family members returned to the gravesite and carefully exhumed the body to examine it for clues as to the status of the person's soul in the afterlife. The length of time the body was required to remain in the ground varied from region to region. In some areas the period was as short as twelve months, while in others, such as Romania, children were disinterred after three years, adults after five, and the elderly after seven. In the Orthodox faith the body's decay was synonymous with the absolution of sins, and the soul could not be free until its former shell had turned to dust. If by some unnatural means the body did not decay, the soul could become trapped within and eventually turn to vampirism for nourishment. If the processes of the body were proceeding naturally and the bones showed to be white, it marked a sure sign that the soul had entered heaven and was now at peace. Once the priests were satisfied that all was well with the deceased, the bones were washed and dressed in fresh linen before receiving a second and final burial.

One of the fundamental differences between the Eastern and Western branches of the church was the very question of the body's incorruptibility and how to interpret the phenomenon. For the Roman Catholic, the process was solely in the hands of God, and if a body remained undecayed after resting in the grave for a period of time it was a sign of sainthood, often accompanied by the fragrance of flowers or other pleasant odors. For the Greek Orthodox, however, it meant the body had become fouled by evil and/or that the church had placed a ban of excommunication upon the deceased so the earth would not receive it. Excommunication was a tool used by the priesthood against those who had committed grievous sins against the church and its authority, and it excluded the offender from the community of the church and therefore from God. This power, the Eastern Church insisted, was invested in them from God, as evidenced in the Book of Matthew (16:19) by the passage "And I will give unto thee the keys of the kingdom of heaven: and whatsoever thou shall bind on earth shall be bound in heaven: and whatsoever thou shall loose on earth shall be loosed in heaven."

For all intents and purposes, excommunication was a punishment worse than death for a Christian and was frequently reserved for unrepentant criminals, heretics, suicides, sorcerers, and as in the case of the Great Schism, political enemies too. Those suffering from this ecclesiastical ban could not enter the kingdom of heaven nor would their body decompose after death unless the sentence was revoked by a pronouncement of absolution over the remains by a priest. In a manuscript discovered in the Church of St. Sophia at Thessalonica, an interesting commentary describes the conditions found in excommunicated bodies and provides insight on how the church interpreted them. Anyone, it says, who had a curse placed upon them or did not fulfill certain obligations to their parents would remain partially undecayed after death. Anyone sanctioned by the church would appear yellow and their fingers would shrivel.

A body that appeared white meant that it had been excommunicated by divine law. Finally, a body that appeared black had been excommunicated by a bishop.

Examples of such ecclesiastical curses litter the early histories of the church, including the tale of a man who converted to Christianity from Islam, but because he remained sinful and impious he was excommunicated by the church. After his death he was buried in the Greek Church of St. Peter the Apostle in Naples, where his body remained undecayed for many years. When the Metropolitan Athansius and several other churchmen visited the site, they preformed a solemn absolution over his and several other undecayed bodies held at the church, all of which immediately turned to dust.

Another was a story recounted by the noted seventeenth-century Cambridge historian Sir Paul Rycaut, who claimed to have received it from a preacher named Sofronia in Smyrna, Turkey. According to the tale, there was once a man infamous for his many crimes living in the Despotate of Morea, which at the time was a southern province in the Byzantine Empire. After yet another heinous crime, the man fled authorities to the isle of Milos in the Aegean Sea, where he died in an excommunicated state. Following his burial, the island's inhabitants began to complain of his apparition returning at night and haunting them in the manner of the bloodthirsty *vrykolaka*. According to custom, the suspected vampire's grave was opened and the body within found to be undecayed and full of fresh blood. Initially the islanders wanted to dismember the corpse and boil the parts in wine to dislodge the evil spirit that had taken residence within, but the man's friends objected and petitioned the church (along with a large sum of money) to grant a reprieve. A letter was then sent to Constantinople begging the Patriarch to grant the deceased an absolution and requesting that the time and date of its performance be written down as proof.

Back on the windswept isle of Milos the coffin had been taken from the grave and filled with grapes, apples, nuts, and other food to sate the fiend's hunger. Suddenly the coffin began to shake and rattle, to the great fear of those gathered nearby, but when they had built up enough courage to open it they found the body had turned to dust. When the letter of absolution arrived from Constantinople, the people were amazed to discover that the time and date of the absolution and the miracle were the same.

This notion of the church's authority over both the spiritual and corporal aspects of its subjects' lives was used in more than just domestic examples and was often heralded as a sign that Christianity was indeed the one true religion. In the eastern approaches to the kingdoms ruled by the Orthodox Church, the presence of Islamic nations meant constant encroachments, skirmishes, and outright warfare. With armies of infidels always at its gates, the church did not hesitate to use the issue of incorruptibility as part of its propaganda campaign against Islamic nations.

In the sixteenth century, the German classical scholar and historian Martin Crusius circulated a report regarding Mehmed II, the Ottoman sultan who conquered Constantinople in 1453. At the time there appeared in the court of Mehmed II a number of men versed in Greek and Arabic literature who were investigating the claims made by the Christian church. After tales of Greek priests halting the decomposition of corpses reached these investigators' ears, the sultan insisted that the Patriarch Maximus of Constantinople produce evidence of their authenticity. Not wanting to incur his new ruler's wrath, Maximus hastily convened a council of priests who managed to produce the undecayed body of a woman who had been excommunicated by the previous patriarch for terrible crimes. Once handed over to the sultan's officers, the body of the woman was placed within a bound coffin marked by the sultan's seal and guarded by his soldiers. After three days, the priests gathered beside it and chanted a liturgy while the patriarch recited an absolution. Following the service, the coffin was opened and the body within found to be nothing more than dust and bones. The sultan was said to be so amazed by this turn of events that he exclaimed to his officers that such proof could only mean that Christianity was the one true religion.

Another tale highlighting the political and religious tensions between Christianity and Islam at the time concerns a bishop who pronounced the ban of excommunication upon a man who died and remained uncorrupted. The bishop, being deceived by Satan, so the story goes, renounced his faith and converted to Islam. The Patriarch of Constantinople summoned the former bishop and requested that he remove the ban so that the man's soul might find release. At first he refused, claiming that it was a Christian matter and since he was no longer a Christian he would have nothing to do with the rites of absolution. The patriarch pleaded nevertheless, and the former bishop relented and performed the rites over the corpse of the excommunicated man, which turned to dust as soon as he was finished. Amazed by what he had just witnessed, he immediately fled to the chief magistrate of the district and related the facts as he had witnessed them. Recanting his Islamic conversion, he proclaimed aloud to all that Christianity was the true religion. Although he was warned by his fellow Turks of the consequences should he continue speaking thus, he only grew bolder in his witnessing. Eventually the former bishop was arrested and executed, but all the while he maintained his faith and was said to have died happily.

A D⊕UBLE-EDGED SW⊕RD

Regardless of its value as a political tool, there were instances in which propagating the belief in vampires also meant taking responsibility for the outcome—and as with any well-sharpened sword, if not used properly the welder could find it cut both ways. In certain isolated incidents, the presence of a suspected vampire in the community was blamed on the local clergy, whose obvious curse, the villagers reasoned, had created the monster. In one story, a bishop was traveling through the Despotate of Morea when he was accosted by highwaymen on a secluded section of road. The robbers quickly relieved the bishop of all his worldly goods and made off, but before too long they began to worry that the man of faith might excommunicate them and therefore doom them to become vampires. Fearing the worst, they reasoned there was only one way to set things right, and so overtaking the bishop once again, they murdered him along the roadway.

A more modern example occurred during the Theriso uprising on the island of Crete in 1905. A native of the municipality of Theriso became gravely ill one day, and it was assumed by many that he was the victim of a curse by the local priest. Friends and relatives of the victim threatened the priest that if he did not remove the curse and the man died that the priest would soon follow. Unfortunately, the man grew worse and died, and true to their word a group gathered before the church, dragged the hapless priest outside, and shot him to death.

Soon after the reports of Arnod Paole and Peter Plogojowitz appeared in newspapers in the early 1700s and the vampire craze reached a fever pitch, the Roman Catholic portion of the church began to lose interest in the topic. The two cases launched a heated debate in the German Lutheran and Catholic universities as to whether vampires truly existed. Cardinal Schtrattembach, the Roman Catholic bishop of Olmütz, turned to Rome for guidance on how the vampire reports flooding in should be handled. Rome then turned the matter over to Archbishop Giuseppe Davanzati, of Trani, Italy, who had spent many years studying the problem and had written an influential work entitled *Dissertazione sopra i Vampiri* on the subject in 1744.

Davanzati, like many others involved in the German debates, had taken a rather skeptical view of the topic and advised Rome that the reports emanating from Eastern Europe were a mixture of superstitious imaginings and latent pagan customs. While these influences in and of themselves may still be the work of the devil, he reasoned, the church's true role should be directed towards the poor soul making the claims rather than the vampire itself. The church found this reasoning to be sound, and from thenceforth adopted it as policy.

While vampires and vampirism waned among the churches of the west, they continued to find support with the Orthodox traditions of the east for some time to come. Even today, cloudy visages of its past stain the more obscure rituals of the Eastern church, even if some of the meaning has been lost, and from time to time news reports crop up detailing an incident among some isolated community regarding a belief in vampires. Throughout its long and storied history, the church's view of vampires has changed according to the age it found itself in, but there is no denying its involvement in the folklore of the creatures.

Yet even as the church encouraged the view that it was the people's champion against all that was evil in the world, somewhere along the way it discovered a powerful and dangerous tool in its struggle against the vampire. A little bit of fear, it quickly learned, went a long way in controlling the masses, and what better way to fill the coffers and bring in the flock each Sunday then to encourage the notion that vampires indeed existed. On the one hand, the church appeared to offer a solution to the vampire plagues and vowed to fight the creatures at every turn, while on the other hand it breathed new life into it for its own ends. Who knows if the legends of the vampire would even exist today if it hadn't been for the church? Ironic that what the church sought to destroy, it only ensured for generations to come.

As a general rule, however, when man meets vampire, one of them will die. While the means whereby vampires kill men are fairly limited, the means whereby men kill vampires are diverse.

—PAUL BARBER, *VAMPIRES, BURIAL, AND DEATH: FOLKLORE AND REALITY*

4

LE+'S GE+ READY +⊕ RUMBLE

Clad in dark sunglasses and a long leather overcoat, the man stood amid the circle of snarling vampires with a sneer of contempt upon his face. Neither side moved for what seemed an eternity until suddenly the lone vampire hunter shrugged off his long overcoat to reveal an arsenal of bristling weaponry. Covered in dark body armor, he sported a Benelli M3 shotgun with a pistol grip, a MAC-10 machine pistol, a bandoleer of silver stakes, and a deadly silver-bladed boomerang, but the killing instrument for which he was best known and feared was the razor-sharp sword of Damascus steel strapped to his back. A vampire snarled, baring her pointed canines, and charged in a blur of speed just as the vampire hunter drew his shotgun and fired. In the chaos that ensued, all hell broke loose as the vampire hunter battled his way through the crowd of vampires in a personal quest for revenge against the beasts that killed his mother.

The 1998 blockbuster movie *Blade* introduced audiences to the fictional vampire hunter of the same name and helped to usher in a new archetype of vampire hunter that reached superhero proportions. Before the dawn of the new vampire hunter, the heroes of most vampire tales and movies usually consisted of more human characters, such as Bram Stoker's Professor Van Helsing, who struggled against the creature with the more traditional weapons of cross and stake. In both cases, the avenging figures were mere protagonists in a fictional work, but the question remains as to how the common villager armed and defended himself against such a deadly foe. If so, then do the vampire hunters that fill our modern movies, comic books, and novels have a basis of reality resting somewhere in history's dark past?

DEADLY DEFENSES

To discover the answers to these and other questions we can turn back to the eyewitness accounts that surfaced during the great vampire scares of the eighteenth century. Although it's easy to lose sight of in the horrific details that fill the reports, it's important to note that they do in fact present two very fascinating sides of the same coin. On one we are given the bloody scenes of death and destruction that best characterize the habits and nature of the undead revenant, while the other offers a glimpse as to just how far a frightened mob will go to stamp out the evil menace.

Cases such as those of Arnod Paole and Peter Plogojow-itz, described in chapter 2, clearly demonstrate how a group of common villagers, armed with only rudimentary shovels, torches, and a handful of wooden stakes, can indeed force the hunter to become the hunted. Turning the tables on one of history's most infamous creatures was by no means an exact science, however, and it was achieved through a variety of methods that varied from culture to culture and depended to a large degree on the religious beliefs of the population and the resources at hand. Make no mistake about it though, in the centuries-old battle against the undead, man was by no means defenseless.

Protective Talismans and Wards

Perhaps one of the oldest weapons at man's disposal was the widespread use of talismans and other wards, ranging any-where from magical amulets and sacred symbols to some of the most ordinary objects the peasants could get their hands on. Objects such as crucifixes, mirrors, horseshoes, scissors, fishing nets, holy water, precious metals, and common herbs were just some of the items topping the list. As different as they may seem, what they all held in common was a supernatural ability to repel evil or bring good fortune.

Two of the most potent wards in the folklore of the vampire are items that can still be found in most household kitchens today and were not only employed against blood-sucking revenants but also witches, demons, and other evil spirits. The first is a simple species of onion known by the Latin name *Allium sativum* or, for the rest of us, garlic. Marked by a distinctively pungent smell, it was first used as a charm among the Egyptians, who hung wreaths of it next to the beds of their children to chase off a type of vampiric night spirit known for stealing the breath of infants as they slept. In China and other parts of Asia, garlic was smeared on the foreheads of children to keep them from falling prey to similar creatures, and in the West Indies it was an important ingredient in magical spells to protect from evil. Amid the lands of Eastern Europe, garlic was eaten as everyday protection against vampires and was rubbed on the doors and windowsills of houses, the gateposts of farms, and the horns of cattle.

If garlic reached a bit of an obsession for some, then at times it could even be taken too far, such as on January 9, 1973, when an article appeared in the London *Times* titled "Immigrant's Fears of Vampires Led to Death." The article described a sixty-eight-year-old Polish man in Stoke-on-Trent named Demitrious Myiciura, who died in his sleep after accidentally choking on a piece of garlic. It appears that he placed a sliver of it in his mouth before going to bed and also smeared it on the bedroom's windowsills and stuffed it in the keyhole of his door. As an added precaution, he placed bags of salt near his head and between his legs. His landlady later told investigators that the man believed vampires were trying to get him.

A second ward, briefly mentioned in the case of the Polish man above, is salt. While generally utilized as a food preservative and seasoning, it's not only the oldest mineral used by man but also essential in sustaining human life as one of the primary electrolytes in the body. In some traditions its powers went even beyond these, and it was placed in the cribs of infants to protect them from evil until they could be baptized or upon coffins before burial to keep evil spirits from entering the corpse. Even in today's world of scientific reasoning and rationalism, glimpses of its former use still remain in the superstition of throwing a pinch of it over the shoulder if a salt shaker is accidentally knocked over.

As with garlic, there were a number of plants and herbs employed as wards against the vampire, including mustard seeds, which were sprinkled on the rooftops of many European homes to keep the creature out. The same effect was achieved in certain South American countries by hanging an aloe plant behind a door. In Bosnia, one interesting ritual, practiced by women when visiting a neighbor's house in which a death had recently occurred, acted not so much as a repellent to vampires but rather as a distraction. Before setting out, a woman placed a small twig of hawthorn in her apron pocket. After her respects were paid to the grieving family, she set out once again for home, and along the way dropped the twig on the road behind her. If the recently deceased neighbor had suffered the misfortune of becoming a vampire and was trying to follow the woman home, it would come across the hawthorn twig lying in the road and spring on it without hesitation, allowing its would-be victim time to escape unharmed.

Another type of ward that found its way into the folklore of the vampire included the use of certain metals such as copper, iron, steel, and silver, which were most often fashioned into amulets or other objects. The more precious the metal, the more power it held over evil—with silver topping the list against both werewolves and vampires, who found its very touch toxic to their system. Silver was particularly favored from ancient times because of its associations with purity and the mysterious powers of the moon, and it was used as an antidote against maladies brought on by evil spirits, including diseases, sicknesses of the mind, and the effects of the evil eye. In some countries, silver nails were used to seal coffins and therefore any vampires or evil spirits trying to escape from within. Because of silver's highly reflective surface, it was also worked in much the same way as a mirror. Since tradition held that revenants had no souls and could not cast reflections or shadows, it was only logical then that a creature of such kind who came across a mirror or similar surface and did not see itself reflected back would immediately become terrified and flee.

Even certain colors played a role in the traditions surrounding the vampire. For instance, though the color red was often linked to the condition of corpses suffering from vampirism, it was also a hue guaranteed to drive them away. In the Slavic countries, peasants frequently tied red ribbons to the horns of their cattle to protect the livestock from vampiric infection, as such an infection could in turn be passed to any humans consuming the meat. Red ribbons were also woven into the hair of women and children to protect them not only from vampires but from the power of the evil eye as well. In Greece the primary color was blue, which was painted on windowsills and door frames to keep the undead from entering the house uninvited. Necklaces of blue beads with the image of an eye were worn in a like manner for a more personal defense.

In some localities the practices that developed to ward off vampires demonstrate more clearly the true desperation that many felt in the face of the vampire threat. For instance, some remedies against vampire attacks included digging up the body of the suspected vampire and covering oneself in its blood or at the very least the dirt from its grave. In the famous cases of Arnod Paole and Peter Plogojowitz, the grisly custom was observed, but unfortunately for the victims in both cases it seemed to have little effect. In parallel traditions the blood or ashes of a cremated vampire could be mixed with wine or baked into bread in the hopes that it would serve as an antidote against the threat. In other areas it was the smoke that resulted from burning the body of the creature that promised a measure of protection, and villagers lined up to pass through the burning cloud of the pyre on such occasions. Vestiges of these practices continued at least into the late nineteenth century in rural areas of Rhode Island and Connecticut, where accounts emerged of families exhuming tuberculosis victims, burning their hearts, and consuming the ashes to protect themselves from a disease they thought very similar to vampirism.

Perhaps the most commonly associated ward in the long struggle against the vampire, thanks in part to its frequent appearance in modern vampire films, is the crucifix of the Christian church. Considered one of the most powerful talismans against evil, its origins actually predate the founding of Christianity by many centuries and has been linked to the worship of sun gods among the Chaldeans, Phoenicians, Egyptians, and others. In the first century BCE, it began appearing on the facades of tombs in Italy as a protective ward and on Roman coins bearing the stamp of Jupiter, the ruler of the gods. In the Christian church the crucifix came to symbolize the sacrifice of Christ and the authority of the church over the world. To the European peasant it was a potent device representing all that was good and divine, and therefore could be used against witches, demons, and vampires, all of whom were forced to flee at the very sight of it.

Even making the sign of the cross, either on the body or in the air with one's hand, carried the power to thwart all manner of evil. During the infamous witch burnings of the Middle Ages, inquisitors repeatedly made the sign of the cross in the presence of suspected witches to counteract any spells they might cast. The use of religious objects wasn't limited to the crucifix, however, and the particular device depended on the beliefs of the culture using them. For example, Shinto seals from holy shrines in Asian folklore were most effective in dealing with vampires from those countries.

Magic Spells and Sacred Sites

Closely related to talismans and other protective wards was the application of magic when fighting vampires. Also known as *sorcery*, the ancient art relies on a series of prescribed actions and words imbued with mystical power to bring about a desired result. In Malaysia, for example, primitive sorcerers developed potent spells against the feared *langsuir*, a demoness similar to Lilith, as in the following fragment:

> *O ye mosquito—fry at the river's mouth,*
> *When yet a great way off ye are sharp of eye;*
> *When near, ye are hard of heart.*
> *When the rock in the ground opens of itself,*
> *Then (and then only) be emboldened the hearts*
> *Of my foes and opponents!*
> *When the corpse in the ground opens of itself,*
> *Then (and then only) be emboldened the hearts*
> *Of my foes and opponents!*

May your heart be softened when you behold me,
By grace of this prayer that I use, called Silam Bayu.
(Summers 2005, 255)

In the more Christianized countries of Europe, acts that suggested any form of magic were often disdained as witchcraft and could therefore be punished by imprisonment, torture, and even death. While many Christians believed magic to be derived from the dark powers of the devil, in truth many of their own practices mirrored that of the supernatural craft or in some cases evolved from it. Reciting the Lord's Prayer, church litanies, or reading aloud from the Bible were methods used to exorcise demons, deflect curses, and drive off vampires. In some customs, spitting on the ground in the presence of a vampire would deter it from attacking—the act being a remnant of pre-Christian times when people believed the soul was in some ways linked to a person's saliva and the action of spitting an offering to the gods for good luck.

In Bulgaria there was one unusual method designed to trap a vampire that incorporated a unique blend of both pagan and Christian elements. A sorcerer, or *djadadjii*, armed with the picture of a saint, would lay in wait for the undead creature to pass by on one of its nocturnal outings and would spring out in ambush with the holy icon before him. The vampire in turn would flee the djadadjii and race about looking for a safe place to hide, but whether it chose the dark corners of a barn or the hollowed-out trunks of trees, the wily sorcerer rooted it out. Eventually the vampire had no other option but to take refuge in a bottle that the djadadjii specially prepared with a fragment of the saint's picture within. Once the vampire was inside the bottle, the sorcerer corked the bottle tight, and after saying the proper prayer cast it into a fire and the vampire would be no more.

In addition to these various forms of magic was a belief that certain physical barriers or sacred sites could not be crossed or trespassed on by vampires. The best example of this is the theory that they could not step foot on consecrated ground. The word *consecrated* means "to associate with the sacred," and was applied to churches, graveyards, and homes blessed by a priest. Remember: corpses suspected of becoming a revenant were not buried in consecrated ground but in isolated areas or crossroads away from the public. Almost as if to counter this belief, however, in most of the reports of vampire infestations handed down over the centuries, the first place frightened villagers looked for the source of the vampire infestation was in their local graveyard.

Another area traditionally off limits to the vampire was a person's home, which the vampire could not enter without first being invited, under the pretext that evil could not enter a person's home unless it was brought in by the owners. Running water was another barrier they could not cross because of the vampire's association with causing droughts. Bloated bodies suspected of vampirism would also float if cast into water, giving the impression that the water was rejecting them. Because of its life-giving properties and numerous biblical references, water was also an element representing purity and could therefore not be touched by the vampire. The only exception in some traditions was that the fiends could cross water at the ebb and flow of the tide. Finally, other magical barriers existed that harkened back to more ancient times, such as the practice of taking twin brothers and having them plow a furrow around a house or village with a team of oxen. As long as the furrow remained intact, no vampire could cross it.

The Rites of Burial

When crucifixes and magic spells failed to do the trick, many Eastern European communities developed complex burial rituals meant to address the continuous threat of the vampire. Since evil spirits relied on decaying corpses as their vehicle to wreak evil upon the world, it only made sense that bodies be prepared in a manner that ensured they did not rise again. Such a process began shortly after a person's death with the ritual cleaning of the body by the family of the deceased. The corpse was normally washed in either water or wine, but in some cases, such as among the Wallachians, it was also rubbed with the lard of a pig killed on St. Ignatius Day. The clothing the person died in was usually exchanged for new garments, with the old set taken out and burned immediately. If the death occurred in the house, it too was cleaned from top to bottom. This ritual cleansing was a means to purify the body and the home and protect the soul, which still lingered about, from the evil influences that might lead to it becoming a vampire.

Once this was accomplished, the arms of the corpse were folded across its chest in the form of a rudimentary cross and the eyes were weighted shut with coins. Not only did the coins prohibit an infected corpse from casting the evil eye, but they were also part of an earlier tradition that believed the soul needed money in the afterlife to pay Charon "the Ferryman of Hades" to transport it across the river Styx and into the land of souls. The mouth of the corpse was stuffed with cloth or wool before being shut, or in some cultures with items such as garlic, gold coins, or religious icons as well. In areas such as Saxony, lemons were used, while in China jade served the same purpose.

The act of stuffing and binding the mouth fulfilled two very important purposes: the first was to prohibit demons and evil spirits from entering the body, while the second ensured the corpse could not begin to feed upon its burial shroud and spread disease. Recently, Italian archeologists unearthed the body of a woman from a mass grave on Lazzaretto Nuovo Island, near the city of Venice, where she had been buried with a small brick deliberately placed between her upper and lower teeth. The 1576 plague victim was suspected of having been a vampire, and gravediggers routinely stuffed bricks in the mouths of such corpses to prevent the spread of the plague.

Other items of significance that were left on dead bodies included shards of pottery or wax crosses bearing the inscription "Jesus Christ Conquers." Among the Greeks a candle known as the *isou* was crafted at the time of the person's death and placed on the chest of the corpse until burial. Once lighted, it was thought to provide enough illumination for the soul so that it would not become lost in the forty days it was required to roam the earth after death.

While the body awaited burial, family and friends kept a constant vigil over it in order to guarantee that the proper respect was being shown and that all the necessary funeral rites were observed. After all, they were the ones who had the most to lose if the person came back as a vampire since traditionally it chose its first victims from among those closest to them in life. Any mirrors in the home were also covered to make sure the wayward soul did not become trapped within them, and clocks were stopped in order to place the soul in a type of suspended state that protected it from the ever-present demonic forces at work. Finally, crosses were painted on the exterior of the house in tar or other substances in a last-ditch effort to seal it from contaminating influences.

When the appointed time for the burial did finally arrive, the utmost care was taken when removing the body from the safety of the home. Often the body was removed through the back door feet first, or a hole was cut in the wall or roof for its removal in the hopes that if the body did rise again it would be unable to find its way back home. Even the route of the procession followed a prescribed pattern, usually traveling from east to west along the path of the sun—and failure to observe the ritual meant the corpse would become cursed along with those accompanying the body. Finally, if the person had lived an upright and moral life, following the precepts of the church, they were eligible for burial in sacred ground consecrated by the church among the family and friends who went before them.

Once the body was in the grave, the local parish priest performed the church rites according to the faith of the deceased, which sometimes included a mass. After the last shovelful of dirt was cast atop the body, food was sometimes left at the grave under the pretense that a well-fed corpse had no need to rise from the dead and sup upon the blood of the living. In some regions, such as Germany, the act was merely symbolic and constituted little more than sprinkling rice or grain over the grave in a token offering. Among those of the Greek Orthodox faith, a supplemental burial was performed after a specified period of time in which the body was disinterred and examined for signs of vampirism. If none existed and the body's process of decomposition seemed natural, the bones were cleaned with boiled water or wine and reburied in a new funeral shroud with all the previous burial customs.

If a person, however, had led an immoral life, was excommunicated by the church, committed suicide, or suffered some breach in burial protocols and there was even the slightest chance they might return as a vampire, means were devised to confuse or deceive the creature with something akin to early psychological warfare. This could in some cases mean simply burying the corpse facing downwards, so that if it attempted to dig its way out (thinking it was right side up) it would instead dig its way deeper into the earth. Often enough this was also a precaution for those later digging up the corpse to examine it for signs of vampirism, as the gaze of the revenant could kill a man or drive him crazy.

In many of the legends surrounding the creatures, they were not only known for their bloodthirsty habits but also for suffering from a touch of obsessive compulsive behavior, which crafty villagers were often quick to capitalize on. Sand and seeds were frequently left within the grave or coffin of the vampire, who in turn could not help but to stop and count each grain at the agonizingly slow pace of one a year. In a similar approach, some bodies were wrapped in fishing net; the vampire felt compelled to untie each and every knot before it could arise, in much the same fashion as with the grain-counting procedure.

Grave Restraints and Corpse Killing

If a few parlor tricks couldn't do the job, then oftentimes cultures found ways to physically restrain or imprison the corpse so that it could not claw its way from the grave. One manner of achieving this was to pin the burial shroud of the corpse to the inside of the coffin and thus restrict its movements. Another, more popular version was simply to bind the arms and legs with leather thongs or ropes. In many areas heavy stones were also laid across the top of the grave, not only to keep scavengers from getting to the body but also to keep the body from getting out of the ground.

One ancient tale of such methods originated in County Derry, in Ireland, after a chieftain named Abhartach, who was renowned for his cruelty, was killed in a battle against a rival clan. Following his burial, Abhartach began reappearing to his kinsmen in search of blood to drink. Time and again the clansmen struck him down with swords and other weapons and reburied the body, but each night he rose again to wreak havoc among the people. At their wit's end, the clan elders finally consulted a local Druid, who advised that they carve a wooden sword from a yew tree, and after striking him down with the sword, bury the corpse upside down with a heavy stone atop the grave. The next night when the vampire appeared again, the people did as the Druid instructed and the bloody chieftain arose no more.

An alternative method included restraining the corpse with the branches of particular trees thought to have extraordinary powers. The aspen, for example, protected people from numerous types of evil because it was thought by some to be the same wood used to make the cross Christ was crucified upon, and so when laid over a grave it bound the vampire within. The Wallachians laid the thorny branches of the wild rose over the body during burial so that if it tried to rise it would become entangled. The Russians, however, preferred to place corpses suspected of vampirism in strong coffins bound with heavy iron bands, which they placed in a special chamber of the church and set a guard upon for a period of time.

Some cultural conventions even espoused ritualistically killing the corpse for a second time. Sharp needles, spikes, or swords were thrust into the ground above the grave in order to impale the body of the vampire should it attempt to dig its way out again. Similarly, in Serbia, after a person died and was taken from the house for burial, the women of the village would gather that night and stick five hawthorn pegs or old kitchen knives in the ground above the body corresponding to the chest, arms, and legs. Another example of the practice can be found among the Morlacks (of modern Croatia), among whom a body suspected of vampirism would be dug up and pricked all over with needles, after which the hamstrings were cut to prevent the corpse from walking again. Other forms of corpse mutilation appeared in places like Transylvania, where exhumed bodies had iron forks thrust into their eyes and heart before reburial upside down.

Even up to the nineteenth century, grisly customs such as these popped up from time to time in places like Romania, where at the conclusion of the funeral rites the coffin was shot with a gun. In fact, to this very day acts such as these continue to surface in the more remote districts of Eastern Europe. On November 24, 1998, for example, a curious article appeared in the Romanian newspaper *Ziua* under a headline translated as "A Gorjean Stuck a Nail through the Heart of Her Dead Lover." The piece went on to explain that Romanian police in the region of Gorj were currently looking for a thirty-five-year-old woman named Vasilica Popescu, who was suspected of desecrating the corpse of her former lover by driving a six-inch nail through his heart. She told reporters that it was an ancient custom in her village and ensured that the heart of the deceased did not start beating again. She continued by stating that while he was alive, her lover routinely performed the same service for many others buried in the village cemetery.

WEAPONS OF WAR

Yet even if all the necessary precautions were taken, an isolated community could still find itself in the deadly grip of a vampire infestation, towards which they had no choice but to take a more direct approach. In circumstances such as these, it was first necessary to identify the source of the vampirism. In most cases this was a simple affair, as the creature could through a little deduction be traced back through the family and friends it chose to make a meal of. All that remained was to follow the body trail back to the grave of the monster and in the full light of day dispatch it with ease. Unfortunately, in the real world, where things are not as easy as they sound, it wasn't always clear who the vampire might be. If it was an invisible spirit or an unrecognized stranger in the community, or if family members were afraid to come forward and admit its identity, other means of identification had to be relied upon.

One method popular in Eastern Europe was as elaborate as it was dramatic. It involved placing a young, virginal boy atop a stallion that had never mated or stumbled and was without blemish. In some versions, the stallion had to be pure white while in others it needed to be completely black. Either way, the horse was set to wander the graveyard of the probable vampire until it reached a grave it refused to cross over even after repeated blows across its flanks. This, then, according to the logic of the times, marked the daylight resting place of the revenant. Other signs included graves that were disturbed by wolves or dogs, who were the natural enemy of the creature, as well as holes the size of a person's finger from which the vampire came and went from the grave. Disturbed coffins, vandalized tombstones, strange mist, and hovering blue flames also pointed to the presence of the vampire.

Wooden Stakes

Once the location of the revenant was rooted out, the average villager had a number of means by which to end the creature's reign of terror. The first included driving a wooden stake through the heart or body of the vampire. While commonly used among the Slavic countries, the origins of the practice may have its roots in Egyptian theology, in which the heart was seen as the seat of the soul, emotions, and intelligence.

The type of wood from which the stake was carved was very important and normally depended on the region where it was being employed. In Russia and the Baltic lands, ash was the popular choice, in Serbia it was hawthorn, while in Poland it was oak. Blackthorn was another wood frequently used in other Christian countries because of its close ties to the crown of thorns Jesus wore at his crucifixion. In some cases the stake could even be made of metal, as was common among the Bulgarians of the medieval period, who heated iron spikes until they were red hot, or the Albanians, who used daggers blessed by a priest.

Commonly, the prescribed approach was to drive the stake through the heart or chest cavity of the corpse, but in some customs it was thrust into the mouth or stomach instead. According to Russian beliefs, it was necessary that the act be committed with a single blow—otherwise a second might reawaken the vampire. This one-blow theory was a constant motif throughout the heroic sagas of Slavic lore, where the hero of the tale could only strike the monster but once.

The act itself served several purposes, including deflating the bloated corpse and releasing the blood trapped within as well as stopping the heart of the vampire from continuing to beat. Underlying this was the even older belief that a stake could pin the corpse to the earth, both so that it could not physically rise and also to create a supernatural link with the earth that would allow the body to finally decompose. Burials during these periods were often conducted without the luxury of a coffin and in a shallow grave scraped out of the hard earth with the simplest of tools. The stake therefore was perhaps the only thing holding the vampire down.

By 1823 the morbid practice of staking suicides became so rampant that the government of Britain was forced to enact laws protecting the bodies of those who died by their own hand, or *felo de se*. Under one such law, the coroner was to "give directions for the private internment of the remains of such a person *felo de se* without a stake being driven through the body of such a person" (Blackstone 1836, 190).

Decapitation

Decapitation, the act of separating the head from the body, was another effective, if gruesome, means of bringing an end to the vampire and was used to a large extent in Germany and the western Slavic countries. Unlike stakes, which were required to be carved from the wood of particular trees, anything could be used to cut the head off of a vampire, from rusty kitchen knives and hatchets to farming sickles and shovel blades. In some traditions, the shovel of a gravedigger or sexton had supernatural powers against vampires—the former because it was used in laying bodies to rest, and the latter because it was a tool used by a man of the church.

Although anyone could perform the deed, local executioners were often called upon to do the job, not only for their proficiency and experience in removing the head from the body but also because in the minds of common people the act was a sort of second execution for the crimes committed by the vampire. Once the head was removed, the mouth was frequently stuffed with garlic and either placed at the feet of the corpse, behind the buttocks, or reburied some distance from the body. The idea was that if a vampire could not see, smell, or chew on its victims, then it posed little threat. Beyond this, decapitation opened the corpse in a way that allowed any evil spirits residing within to quickly find their way out.

Fire

A third tactic involved the complete and utter destruction of the corpse or at least certain key parts, such as the heart and other vital organs, by fire. This usually meant dragging the corpse from its grave and onto a pyre of wood sometimes soaked with pitch or other flammables. Although the type of wood was unimportant, whenever possible the lumber was collected from trees and shrubs bearing thorns, which as seen earlier carried certain biblical connotations. Once the match was struck, it then became necessary to capture and burn any creatures escaping the flames regardless of their size or shape, because they might just be the vampire in disguise. In many areas it was also crucial that no scrap or fragment of the body survive the flames, as the vampire could rejuvenate itself from the smallest portion. Once the cremation was complete, the ashes were collected and tossed into a swiftly flowing river so that they could not be used by sorcerers in the creation of evil magic.

Burning the vampire's remains not only destroyed the vehicle by which it walked the earth but also purified the essence of the corpse. The flame, as history proved again and again, was one of the favorite tools of the church when it came to defeating evil and was how it often "rehabilitated" those accused of witchcraft or sorcery. Yet even before the church adopted the practice, fire was a magical element used during pagan times as a central theme in rituals of cleansing, warmth, and protection. However, early man learned quickly that cremation was a difficult process, given the density of muscle and bone and the high water content of the body. Today's crematories use ovens that reach temperatures as high as 2,000 degrees Fahrenheit, and they still require up to a half-hour, depending on the weight and mass of the corpse, to reduce a corpse to ashes. Even then, a quantity of bone remains, which must be ground into dust until all that is left of the human body consists of between four to eight pounds of nondescript material.

To alleviate the problems inherent in such a process, including the vast quantities of wood and manpower necessary to feed the flames for what could amount to days on end, some cultures turned to forms of symbolic cremation instead.

In Bulgaria, for instance, a corpse thought to possess the spirit of a vampire was surrounded by a ring of flammable material. Villagers then lined up to take a hot coal, which they cast behind them in a gesture meant to drive the evil spirit away. In Serbia a similar practice existed whereby only the hair of the corpse was singed with a candle.

Sunlight

According to modern moviemakers, sunlight was a powerful weapon used to reduce vampires to a pile of ash, but as we learn so very often, Hollywood rarely gets it right. The truth of the matter is that nowhere in the folklore or the historical texts does this theory actually appear. Instead, the prevailing belief among the Serbians and others was that vampires became helpless when exposed to the rays of the sun, falling into a type of catatonic slumber or quasi-death trance. This helped explain why vampires appeared as simple inanimate corpses when villagers dug them up and ripped them from their coffins.

To help account for the condition, it was surmised that since vampires were primarily night stalkers that derived their infernal powers from the darkness, it only made sense that daylight would prove their weakness. There is no precedent that they turned to dust or exploded into flames, however, and perhaps the first suggestion of this belief didn't appear until F. W. Murnau's 1922 German film *Nosferatu*. On the contrary, in some traditions, like those found among the Russians, vampires could move about on sunny afternoons just like the rest of us.

THE VAMPIRE OF BRESLAW

There were, of course, many other ways in which to slay a vampire, including excision of the heart, dismemberment of the body, burial under a gallows, piercing by sword, and immersion in water—and often more than one method was used in conjunction with others. The exact methodology again depended on the region, religious practices, and resources of the people, and each province or ethnic group seemed to enjoy putting their own little spin on the act. A classic example of just how these methods were used "in the field" can be found in English philosopher Henry More's 1653 edition of *An Antidote against Atheism—or—An Appeal to the Natural Faculties of the Minde of Man*. In this work appears the tale of a wealthy shoemaker in the town of Breslaw (today known as Wroclaw, a major city, in what is now southwestern Poland), who on September 20, 1591, committed suicide by slitting his own throat with a knife in the garden behind his house.

Given the religious prohibitions against such an act, his family conspired to hide the suicide by covering up his wounds with the burial shroud in order to fool the examining priest into thinking that he had suffered a stroke instead. Perhaps the family's wealth played a part in making a few heads turn the other way also, but regardless of how the deception was carried off the shoemaker was buried in the graveyard with all the solemn rites of the church. If the family thought the matter was laid to rest, however, they quickly found they were mistaken, and rumors began spreading that his death was not the work of natural causes after all.

Talk of the shoemaker's death continued to circulate in Breslaw until the local authorities stepped in and began questioning family members, who eventually broke down and confessed
their duplicity. While the town's council gathered to discuss the
matter, the shoemaker's widow began complaining to any who
might listen that the recent confessors were no more than mali-
cious liars bent on staining her late husband's reputation. Even
worse, she promised to take her case all the way to the Kaiser if
necessary to protect her family's honor. Initially the council was
reluctant to have their town overrun with the government officials such a complaint would bring and voted to dismiss any
charges of wrongdoing against the shoemaker's family. Before
the smoke cleared, however, new rumors arose that the apparition of the shoemaker was roaming the cobbled streets of Breslaw at night, terrorizing the inhabitants.

Witnesses to the attacks claimed that "those that were
asleep it terrified with horrible visions; those that were waking it would strike, pull or press, lying heavy upon them like
an *Ephialtes*: so that there were perpetual complaints every
morning of their last night's rest through the whole
town ... For this terrible *Apparition* would sometimes stand
by their bed-sides, sometimes cast itself upon the midst of
their beds, would lie close to them and pinch them, that not
only blue marks, but plain impression of the fingers would
be upon sundry parts of their bodies in the morning" (Summers 2003, 134).

At the outset of these bizarre new rumors, friends and
family of the shoemaker rallied to stifle the murmurings, but
as time went on the claims only became worse—until a thick
blanket of fear lay over the town of Breslaw. Each night the
people locked and bolted their doors, and it was said that even

when groups gathered for protection the vampire appeared, and after assaulting its intended victim vanished back into the night from whence it came.

Eventually, town officials became so distressed by these events that they felt they had no recourse but to exhume the body of the shoemaker and dispatch the vampire that it had become. On April 18, 1592, the grave was uncovered under the supervision of the town magistrate and examined for signs of vampirism. As the growing mob of local curiosity seekers gathered at the scene, many claimed that they noticed a magic mark on the big toe of the corpse and that the "body was found entire, not at all putrid, no ill smell about him saving the mustiness of the Grave-cloaths, his joints limber and flexible, as in those who are alive, his skin only flaccid, but a more fresh grown in the room of it, the wound of his throat gaping, but no gear nor corruption in it ..." (Summers 2003, 135).

For an entire week the body was left exposed in the grave, with many coming to see the "Breslaw Vampire." Finally the body was taken and reburied under the town's hanging gallows, but the vampire's attacks only became more frequent and violent. This time it was the widow herself who came to the magistrate and begged that something be done to end the vampire's attacks upon the town and finally put her poor husband's soul to rest.

The body was again unearthed, only this time to be found even more bloated with fresh blood. The local hangman was ordered to decapitate the corpse and dismember the remainder of the body, after which the heart was removed through its back and shown to be full of blood. The various pieces were then burned to ash and collected in a sack to be disposed of in a nearby river. Following these measures the vampire ceased to trouble the town, but other accusations continued to plague the shoemaker's family, including claims that one of their deceased servants began rising from the dead as well. In the story she appeared to some as a woman and to others as a dog, cat, hen, or goat. In the end she too was treated in much the same manner as her former master, and as the story goes, was never seen again.

THE FIRST VAMPIRE HUNTERS

While frenzied mobs of villagers tore bodies from their graves and hacked them to bits, another colorful character entered the mythology of the vampire, one who bears a resemblance, however slight, to the archetype of the modern vampire hunter many are familiar with in today's books and movies. Although the professional vampire hunters that surfaced in Europe during this period did not have access to fancy Hollywood props such as steel samurai swords and guns that shoot ultraviolet bullets, they were nonetheless just as flashy and dramatic as anything on the silver screen.

Take, for instance, the *dhampir* of the Balkans, who were the result of a union between a male vampire and a living woman. Even as children they possessed extraordinary powers against the undead and were noted for their large heads, untamed black hair, and the uncanny fact that they had no shadows. Many dhampir were considered powerful sorcerers and were called upon if villagers suspected a vampire in their midst. Once they arrived in the infested township, they frequently made a great show of hunting the vampire, which they claimed only they could see because it was invisible to all others. First a dhampir took off his shirt, which was of course a magical shirt, and scoured the town looking through one sleeve as if it were a telescope. Many times they punctuated the performance with a description of the invisible bloodsucker, and although the crowd was allowed to *ooh* and *ah* and even clap when appropriate, no one was permitted to speak but the dhampir.

Once the vampire was securely in his sights, the dhampir pulled a magic gun from his belt and fired it into the air, announcing with great fanfare that the vampire was now dead. Sometimes the dhampir followed this by pouring water, just for good measure, on the spot where the vampire met its end. Once the hunt was over, the dhampir was paid for his services and traveling expenses, and then quickly skedaddled before anyone was the wiser. Business was so good in fact that many dhampir claimed to have the ability to pass their powers on to their sons, making it a family business. One town was even famous for the large number of families descended from *vrykolakas*, or vampires, that lived there. These families were said to have the ability to slay those vampires they were related to, and although they were shunned in public they were often sought after in private.

Similar to the dhampir were the *Sabbatarians*, who were called that because they were born on the Sabbath, which in the Orthodox faith falls on Saturday. Gifted from birth, these individuals not only had power over vampires but ghosts and other evil creatures as well, which, like the dhampir, only they could see. Stories claim that their powers were so great that vampires fled at the mere sight of them and that twin Sabbatarians were accompanied by a familiar in the form of a spectral dog, which they used to hunt their undead prey. Other odd traditions state that Gypsy Sabbatarians, for instance, wore their underwear inside out, which they swore acted as a potent vampire repellent.

Another type of vampire hunter was found among the Croats in the form of a powerful shaman known as a *kresnik*, whose spirit left his body at night in the shape of a white animal and prowled the village hunting vampire spirits, or *kudlaks*, who appeared as black animals. When the two met, they battled until daybreak, at which time the vampire was forced to retreat back to its grave in defeat. In many villages the kresnik's protective presence was essential for good harvests, long life, and general happiness.

As we have seen in this chapter, the common villager was not at all defenseless against the vampire and armed himself with a deadly array of weaponry. This in turn gave rise to a number of strange and gruesome practices affecting many aspects of the average peasant's life, from protective talismans and magic to how the body was prepared at death. In the midst of this turmoil, a professional class of undead exterminators stepped into the fray to fight the scourge of the vampire (and in the process lighten a few pockets as well) and helped color the image of the vampire hunter we have today.

Some are born to sweet delight, Some are born to endless night.

WILLIAM BLAKE, *AUGURIES OF INNOCENCE*

5

LEGENDS ⊕F BL⊕⊕D

While the very name *Dracula* and the mystery that surrounds his grave at Snagov Monastery conjure up terrifying questions in our search for the real vampire, it is perhaps important that we pause for the moment and return to the "scene of the crime" to examine further evidence that promises to add yet another layer to this dark riddle. In the process we'll explore more of the true history of Dracula, along with several other well-documented figures from the past accused of such atrocities against their fellow man that their names alone bring to mind images of cruelty, torture, sadism, and bloodlust. During their lifetimes these violent men and women were greatly feared by all who crossed their path, and when their bodies had finally disappeared back into the cold earth their memories were so lasting that they became infused into the folklore of the vampire and they themselves became legends of blood.

In 1933, when the crypt at Snagov Monastery proved to be empty of all but a few bones and broken bits of pottery, it must have at first seemed to Dinu Rosetti and George Florescu that they had reached the end of their quest for the legendary grave of Dracula. Yet for these two intrepid archeologists, the work continued on, and as the days passed and further excavations progressed within the ancient chapel, additional finds added yet more clues to the mystery of the empty grave.

Upon carefully examining the rest of the building's interior, the team stumbled on a curious stone slab to the right of the chapel's heavy wooden doors that closely resembled the one marking the empty grave they had previously uncovered. On removing the stone they discovered that it concealed a second crypt identical in both size and shape to the first. The only difference between it and the first was that, as the weighty cover stone was lifted from the grave, Rosetti and Florescu were elated to find this one was occupied.

Deep within the cool recesses of its brick and mortar-lined interior lay a rotting coffin, and inside that the headless body of a man dressed in the red and yellow remnants of a nobleman's garments. Over the body lay a tattered cloth of purple with gold embroidery and to one side a crown intricately shaped and fitted with stones of turquoise.

Although most of the objects had long ago deteriorated beyond recognition, a battered cup, a belt buckle of gold, and other remains were removed to the City of Bucharest History Museum for further study. Also discovered sewn into the folds of the occupant's cloak was a small jeweled ring resembling the type given by ladies of high status to favored knights victorious in tournament. For Rosetti and Florescu, who had studied surviving portraits and eyewitness accounts of the infamous prince, the clothing and objects found in the grave were a dead match for those belonging to Dracula. Dracula's father, Vlad II Dracul, just happened to acquire such objects after successful bouts in a tournament of arms following his initiation into the Order of the Dragon at Nuremberg on November 8, 1431. Later he bequeathed these trophies, along with his prized Toledo sword, to his son Dracula, who was at the time a prisoner of the Turks.

Yet while the archeologists were convinced they had discovered the true and final resting place of Vlad Dracula Tepes, others in the scientific community were still unsure about the find. After reviewing the evidence collected at Snagov Monastery, subsequent scholars and historians pointed out that although the corpse did indeed appear to be that of a nobleman from the middle of the fifteenth century, its location in the chapel was not in keeping with Orthodox traditions. Given its distance from the altar and the fact that there was no inscription upon the stone bearing the identity of its occupant, the lonely grave in the corner of the chapel did not seem a fitting place for a Wallachian prince who at one time was both the monastery's patron and its protector.

In response, the archeologists argued that the coffin may have in fact been originally placed in the first grave near the altar but then, for one reason or another, was secretly exhumed and moved to the second. One of the monastery's abbots could have felt uneasy about having the body of such an evil man so close to the holy altar of God and therefore repositioned the coffin farther away near the door. In an added bit of poetic justice, by placing him near the chapel entrance it allowed the subjects he once crushed under his iron heel to now trample over his remains on their way to worship God.

While his cruel and bloodthirsty reputation may have helped determine the fate of his burial, an even stronger factor could have been his decision to convert to Roman Catholicism shortly before his death. In the eyes of the Orthodox Church, such a move branded him a heretic—making it a violation of church law to inter his body at the altar's base. This may also account for why the grave was unmarked or why no murals or icons of the monastery's former patron existed in the chapel.

Supporters of what we'll call the "musical graves" theory surmise that the transfer occurred either when the monastery came under the control of Greek monks in the 1700s or by order of Metropolitan Filaret II, who headed the Romanian church in 1792. In either case neither the monks nor the patriarch himself bore any love for the memory of the oppressive tyrant. Others claim a third suspect might have been the monks who resided in the monastery in the 1800s and who moved the body to avoid looting by peasants from nearby villages just before the island was abandoned by the holy order.

More than forty years after the initial discovery of the unknown nobleman, a monk residing in the Snagov chapel told reporters in 1975 that he was convinced that Dracula's remains still lay within the grave near the altar and that the original archeologists simply did not dig down far enough. Nobility and other important personalities, he noted, were generally buried very deep, and tricks such as false graves and other disguises were often used to foil grave robbers in search of loot.

Following the release of the story, Raymond T. McNally, a professor of Russian and Eastern European history at Boston College, and Romanian academic Radu Florescu, the nephew of George Florescu, petitioned the Romanian government for permission to reopen the grave and investigate the monk's claims. Unfortunately, their request, along with subsequent others, was denied by officials on the grounds that the chapel's foundations were weakened by earthquakes in 1940 and 1977. To dig within the confines of the chapel at Snagov, the officials claimed, posed a serious threat to both the structural integrity of the ancient building and the safety of those undertaking the excavation. The search for definitive proof of Dracula's resting place would have to wait.

The question then remains as to what Rosetti and Florescu really found on that lonely island in 1933. Did they in fact lay to rest the mystery of the empty grave with the discovery of the headless corpse, or did the ever-elusive clues needed to identify the body only add new layers to the riddle of Dracula's tomb? Who was really buried in the Snagov chapel, and did the spirit of Dracula still roam the lands he once ruled—moving through the ruins of his crumbling castles or lingering among lost battlefields where his sword once tasted the blood of his enemies?

SON OF THE DRAGON

Here begins a very cruel, frightening story about a wild bloodthirsty man, Prince Dracula. How he impaled people and roasted them and boiled their heads in a kettle and skinned people and hacked them to pieces like cabbage. He also roasted the children of mothers and they had to eat the

children themselves. And many other horrible things are
written in this tract and in the land he ruled.

—FROM THE FRONTISPIECE OF A PAMPHLET
PRINTED IN NUREMBERG IN 1499 BY AMBROSIUS HUBER

Sultan Mehmed II reined his magnificent stallion to a halt
with a swift flick of his wrist, just as he and his bodyguards of
elite Janissaries (infantry units) topped the tree-lined ridge.
Below him stretched a small valley and just beyond that another sloping ridge. He was only twenty-seven leagues north
of Dracula's fortified capital of Tirgoviste, which according
to his spies was even now being frantically manned with
troop and cannon in preparation for a siege against him.

Turning his mount, the sultan looked back into the for-
ested valleys from which he had just traveled and watched his
army of over 100,000 men struggling through the dense trees
and marshy ground. Like one long, serpentine beast, the
great troop moved, comprised of Arabian calvary in white
turbans, *azab* spearmen in robes of red and green, Janissary
shock troops in long mail tunics, the *beshlis* with their deadly
firearms, and slave soldiers known as *sipahis* who hoped to
win their freedom if they survived the campaign. Struggling
to keep up in the boggy ground, heavy cannon and supply
wagons followed, mixed with the sick and wounded strag-
glers who had fallen behind.

In 1453, only ten years before, the Turkish Sultan Mehmed
II had, at the age of twenty-one, sacked the Christian city of
Constantinople and broken the back of the Byzantine Empire
for good, sending waves of panic throughout the Western
world. Now his once-glorious army found themselves wearily
trampling through a rugged landscape filled with dark forests

and impenetrable marshes in order to punish the Wallachian prince Dracula and his boyar noblemen for raiding lands that belonged to the Ottoman Empire.

As his army left Constantinople and pushed to cross the Danube River, his military advisors were confident that the sultan's forces, which outnumbered those of Dracula's more than four to one, would make quick work of the infidels and transform the vassal state of Wallachia into a new Turkish province. Yet from the beginning of the campaign the enemy refused to meet him in direct battle, choosing to rely instead on lightning-quick raids to the army's flanks and rear. They had also adopted a scorched-earth tactic, burning crops, poisoning wells, and depopulating the countryside ahead of his advance for miles to come. Hunger and thirst now consumed them all, and while the sultan sent foragers farther afield to gather food, they increasingly fell prey to the prince's forces.

The worst of the fighting occurred just a few nights before while the Turkish army lay encamped. Mehmed remembered waking in the darkness of his tent to the sounds of clashing steel and the screams of dying men. Grabbing his scimitar, he rushed out only to be immediately surrounded by his personal guards. Flares lit the sky and tents blazed as his men battled against an attack force of knights, led by Dracula himself, who using the darkness made a desperate charge into the camp killing all in their path. If the enemy had not mistaken the tents of two of his viziers, Mahmud and Issac, for his own and concentrated their attack there, the sultan knew he might not be alive this day. While initially many of his troops fled in panic, screaming "the *Kazıklı Voyvoda* has come," it was his beloved Janissaries who rallied and forced the attackers to retreat. Many of his men died that night under the sword and lance of his enemy, but now that they were in reach of Dracula's capital it would all be over soon.

An officer of the advance guard quickly galloped up the ridge towards the sultan's position, breaking his thoughts.

"Your highness…" he breathlessly exclaimed as he came to a stop and bowed low in his saddle. "The advance has stalled just over the next ridge … there's something you must see, my lord."

There was terror in the man's eyes, making Mehmed grip the hilt of his scimitar tightly.

"Very well then, lead on," the sultan barked, spurring his horse forward, and the armored troop descended into the valley and up the opposite slope. Upon cresting the rise, the whole party came to a stop as if they had crashed into an invisible barrier. The horses rose on hind legs and cried out in fear, and it took all the strength the riders possessed to keep them from pure blind panic.

Before the sultan and his men lay a scene so horrific that even the most battle-hardened of his officers shuddered in dread amazement. Below them on a vast plain spread a forest of 20,000 stakes placed at various heights, each with the decaying carcass of a Turkish captive impaled upon it. The smell of rotting flesh filled the air as carrion birds circled, screeching and fighting over the ghastly feast. This was the work of the Impaler, and for the sultan it was too much to bear.

"I cannot take the land of a man who could do such a thing," he said almost to himself as the last of his resolve melted away. "It will be dark soon and we must camp, but tomorrow we return to our own lands and away from this accursed place."

That night the Turkish army dug a deep trench around their encampment to keep out the Impaler, and the next day the soldiers of the great Ottoman Empire began to retreat back across the Danube River.

Vlad III Dracula was born in the heavily fortified town of Sighisoara, Transylvania, on a cold winter night in 1431—the same year Joan of Arc was burned at the stake for witchcraft. His father, Vlad II, was an exiled contender for the throne of Wallachia, a region bordering eastern Transylvania in what is now part of Romania, while his mother was the Princess Cneajna of Moldavia. That same year his father traveled to the city of Nuremberg, where he was initiated into the Order of the Dragon, founded in 1408 by the Hungarian King Sigismund to oppose the spread of the Turkish Ottoman Empire into Christian lands. To honor his new allegiance, Vlad II took the name *Dracul*, which in Romanian means both "dragon" and "devil." His infant son, Vlad III, was therefore given the surname Dracula, which can be translated into "son of the dragon" or, more ominously, "son of the devil."

Five years later, in 1436, Vlad II Dracul ascended the throne of Wallachia over the bodies of his main rivals, the House of Danesti, who were aligned with Hungarian interests. Dracula, like any young prince of the era, spent his days with Greek and Romanian tutors studying geography, mathematics, science, and languages, as well as the arts of warfare and combat. Yet even in these early days the young prince exhibited a dark fascination for the macabre, and it's noted that he took great pleasure in watching criminals being led from their cells to his father's castle courtyard to be hanged. When Dracula was twelve, his father shifted policies and allied himself with his sworn enemy, the Turks, against the greater threat of Hungarian aggression. In return for Turkish support, Vlad II Dracul consented to pay tribute to the sultan, part of which included sending his sons Dracula and Radu to the Ottoman court as royal hostages to ensure his loyalty.

It was during his stay among the Turks from 1444 to 1448 that Dracula's propensity for cruelty and bloodlust was further shaped and refined by the various methods of torture and execution he learned from his captors. One of his favorites was that of impalement, which he later used to such great effect that it earned him the title *Kazıklı Voyvoda*, "the Impaler prince," among his enemies. A stout pole or stake was sharpened at one end and driven into the rectum or side of the condemned person, who was then hoisted into the air. Gravity and the victim's own struggles forced the stake deeper into the body, slicing into organs and eventually working its way out through the sternum, mouth, or the top of the head in an excruciatingly painful process that could take days to kill the victim. In some cases the stakes were oiled to avoid piercing vital organs and to prolong the process, and even infants were sometimes impaled upon the very stakes that protruded from their mother's dying breast.

In December of 1447 the boyars, or landholding nobles, of Wallachia rebelled against Vlad II Dracul and assassinated him in the marshes of Balteni, near Bucharest, to make way for the return of his old nemesis, the House of Danesti. Dracul's eldest son and immediate heir to the kingdom, Mircea, was also captured and blinded with red-hot iron stakes before being buried alive. To keep the Hungarian throne from using the turmoil as a pretext to invade Wallachia, the

Turks released the now seventeen-year-old Prince Dracula, who with the support of Turkish cavalry and other troops led a bold and successful coup to recapture his homeland. The son of the dragon had finally returned, and this time he was out for blood.

Over a period spanning the next twenty-eight years, Vlad III Dracula ruled Wallachia on three separate occasions in 1448, 1456 to 1462, and for a brief two months in 1476. Upon first taking the throne, Dracula was met by a land wracked with internal conflicts, rampant crime, a failing agricultural system, and an unstable economy. Wasting no time, the young prince enacted a series of long and bloody reforms aimed at consolidating his power and ridding the land of potential threats to Wallachia's stability. One of his first acts was to avenge the deaths of his father and brother and exterminate the greedy boyars who lined their pockets with foreign gold at the expense of the people.

In what can only be seen as a bit of brilliant Machiavellian maneuvering, Dracula invited all the wealthy boyar households to an Easter celebration as a sign of his reconciliation and forgiveness. At the end of the festivities, as the nobles left one by one, soldiers loyal to Dracula seized and placed them in chains. Once all the guests were rounded up, Dracula immediately impaled the old and infirm among them on tall spikes. The rest he force-marched under guard for two weary days until they reached the ruins of Poenari Castle, sitting high above the Arges River gorge. Here he planned to rebuild the once-imposing fortress and would use the nobles as labor. Men, women, and children were brutally worked until their once gaily colored Easter clothing became rags and fell from their limbs. Many died in the construction either from falls into the gorge or from pure exhaustion, but in this one bold stroke Dracula achieved several important aims: he effectively rooted out any remaining boyar resistance to his rule; he seized the boyars' wealth and lands, giving him an instant source of capital to buy loyal followers; and it gave him the dispensable workforce he needed to compete his castle stronghold.

Once most of Dracula's political opponents lay either broken among the rocks at the base of his castle or rotting atop blood-drenched stakes, the now-seasoned prince could turn his attention to other matters, but as with all his measures, Dracula moved with a tyrant's callous brutishness. In one example of Dracula's particular brand of justice, a Gypsy was caught stealing in a nearby village and thrown into the dungeon. When relatives of the man came to beg for his release, Dracula had the thief boiled in a pot and forced his relatives to eat the body, after which he had them impaled for the crime of cannibalism.

On another occasion, the prince became distressed that his land was becoming overrun with vagabonds and other undesirables who drained the countryside of its resources and burdened the people. Taking a page from his earlier playbook, Dracula held a great feast at his castle and invited all the poor, lame, sick, and homeless in his kingdom to attend. Once the riotous guests filled their bellies to the point of bursting and their flagons to the point of drunkenness, Dracula stood before the assembly and asked if after all this there was anything else they might want. They in their joviality answered back that their lord had now given them everything they could ever ask for. This appealed to Dracula's ironic nature, and with a wolfish grin he exited the hall, locked the doors behind him, and set the place ablaze—killing all inside.

Yet of all the bloody acts Dracula committed, it is perhaps his raid on the Transylvanian town of Brasov in April of 1459 that received the most attention. Brasov was primarily a German Saxon town whose merchants were competing with native Wallachians for trade in the region. In order to break their monopoly, Dracula sacked the town with his army. After blasphemously looting the local church, his forces led thousands of the town's people outside the city walls and impaled them. When a nobleman in his routine complained of the stench, the prince had him impaled on a taller stake so that he would be above the smell.

During many of the mass impalings he ordered it was said that Dracula liked to have a table set amid the stakes where he could dine and casually watch his victims writhing in agony. Adding to the tales it was also claimed that his servants collected into a bowl the blood that ran down the stakes, which Dracula frequently dipped bread into and ate. Although the latter addition of blood-drinking may have been an invention by his German enemies to demonize him to the rest of Europe, the stories of his atrocities and allegations of blood-drinking began appearing in pamphlets across the continent even in his own lifetime. Two of the most famous examples that survive to this day were printed in Nuremberg in 1499 and Strasbourg in 1500 and show the well-dressed prince at a table dining before a forest of impaled bodies, while his soldiers hack and boil other victims in a caldron.

It is estimated by some that during the course of Dracula's reign he impaled between 40,000 and 100,000 victims, a figure that does not take into account those he killed by other means.

By the year 1462, Prince Dracula began to chafe under the heavy yoke of the Ottoman Empire, and goaded by calls from Pope Pius II for a new crusade against Turkish aggression, he decided to break his alliance with Sultan Mehmed II. Since he could ill afford to battle along two fronts simultaneously, his first move was to seek an uneasy peace with his former enemies to the west: the Hungarian dynasty and the German Saxons of Transylvania. Having achieved a truce with his neighbors and even promises of support from the Hungarians, Dracula formulated a plan to draw the sultan into armed conflict. He began by ceasing his annual shipment of tribute in the sum of 10,000 ducats to the Turks, claiming that years of constant warfare with his neighbors left him no time to deliver on these earlier promises.

He next seized any Turkish merchants or officials unfortunate enough to cross into his lands and impaled them on stakes. In one well-recorded incident, Turkish emissaries arrived at his court to inquire as to the prince's true intentions and remind him of his debt to the sultan. When Dracula asked them to remove their turbans in his presence, something he knew they could not do, the diplomats refused, citing that it was against their customs. Enraged, Dracula had them held while his men nailed the turbans to their heads with tiny metal pins. He sent them, insulted and bleeding, back to their master as a clear message of his intentions. Finally, Dracula began raiding Turkish settlements across the Danube River, burning and pillaging without mercy. The sultan was furious by these acts of open hostility, and Dracula now had his war.

In the initial phases of the campaign, Dracula's forces seemed unstoppable as they crossed into Turkish Bulgaria, laying waste to the countryside; but while many of the Christian kingdoms he hoped to draw into the conflict praised his efforts, none, including the Hungarians, came to his aid. The sultan in the meantime was committed to other fronts in Asia but finally managed to turn his attention to the fighting along his western borders, and with a massive army he invaded the tiny kingdom of Wallachia. Over the course of the conflict, Dracula's smaller force struck repeatedly at the lumbering Turkish army with lightning-quick raids and guerilla tactics designed to wear their opponent down.

By the time the sultan limped back home with his broken army, it's estimated that almost one-third of his original forces were lost to the fighting. While Dracula was momentarily seen as the victor of the contest, he too suffered tremendous losses and desertions that chipped away at his forces until there was little left save a small group of loyal bodyguards hiding in the mountains. More damaging, however, was that dissident boyars weary of his harsh tactics began turning against him in favor of his brother Radu, who was still in service to the sultan.

Later that year, Dracula's war finally came to an end when he was ambushed and taken captive by the soldiers of King Matthias Corvinus of Hungary, who had initially pledged to assist Dracula in his struggle against the Turks. Charges of secretly seeking a truce with the Ottomans were trumped up with forged documents, and for the next twelve years Prince Dracula remained a prisoner of the Hungarians at Visegrád, near Buda. No stranger to captivity, Dracula managed to win the favor of King Matthias during his stay, even marrying the king's cousin Ilona Szilagyi and converting to Roman Catholicism, the religion of the Hungarian court. In 1475 Dracula was officially released and accompanied the king in fighting against the Turks in Bosnia, where he proved himself once again a fierce and merciless fighter. Impressed by his prowess in battle and looking to put a pro-Hungarian back in charge of Wallachia, Corvinus placed Dracula at the head of a Hungarian army in 1476 and gave him the green light to win back his kingdom.

With his new fighting force, Dracula once again entered the lands of his father to face the Turks, but after several months of brutal fighting the legendary Impaler Prince fell in battle. Details of his end are sketchy at best and depend on who is telling the story, but the most popular claim is that he was killed in battle by his own men. The story goes on to say that he slew five of his attackers with his own sword before being brought down with the arrows and lances of his adversaries.

While it's true that Dracula had many enemies on both sides of the border eager to spill his blood, it is perhaps the contemporaneous chronicler Jakob Unrest who gives us our clearest view of the prince's last moments. He recounts that in the winter of 1476 Dracula's forces were attacked by a much larger group of four thousand Turks near Snagov Monastery, and that Dracula was assassinated by his personal servant in a small, lonely clearing among the marshes in a forest near Bucharest. His head was then cut off and spirited away to Constantinople, where the sultan displayed it on a pole so that all might see that the dreaded son of the dragon was finally dead.

BL⊕⊕DY C⊕UN✝ESS

When my men entered Csejthe Manor, they found a girl dead in the house; another followed in death as a result of many wounds and agonies. In addition to this, there was

also a wounded and tortured woman there; the other vic-
tims were kept hidden away where this damned woman
prepared these future martyrs.
—LETTER FROM GYÖRGY THURZÓ TO HIS WIFE (DECEMBER 30,
1610), AS QUOTED IN KIMBERLY L. CRAFT, *INFAMOUS LADY: THE*
TRUE STORY OF COUNTESS ERZSÉBET BÁTHORY

The company of men made their way grimly through the darkness wrapped against the winter cold in heavy woolen cloaks. Their leader, Lord György Thurzó, the Palatine of Hungary, paused for a moment as the silent troop continued to file by. Peering through the lightly falling snow to the mountain slopes above, the dark shape of an imposing castle perched like a dangerous beast threatening to devour them. Yet for Lord Thurzó and his men, what waited for them behind those ancient walls that night would be something they would never forget.

When the men finally reached the castle's massive wooden doors, they were surprised to find them open and unguarded. Creeping inside the smoky, torchlit hall, they spied the body of a young servant girl lying in a pool of her own blood.

One of the men moved forward and examined the corpse. "She is from the castle, my lord," he whispered. "It looks as if she has been stabbed and beaten many times."

The men hurriedly discarded their cloaks and drew their swords.

"I want every inch of this damned castle searched," Thurzó growled. "But most importantly, I want the countess."

As the men advanced farther into the castle, what followed was a confusing nightmare of horrid sights and sounds. Two more unfortunate women were found tortured and discarded: one long past help while the other clung weakly to life with shallow, ragged breaths. Thurzó stopped long enough to order two of his men to carry the survivor back down the mountain to the village below while the rest continued onward. Deeper into the castle's depths the men were halted by anguished screams coming from behind a bolted door. Bursting through the wooden barrier, they were shocked by the sight of three old women and a disfigured boy gleefully stabbing to death a young naked girl stretched on a table. In one corner of the chamber another small girl huddled with her head in her hands awaiting the same fate. Rushing forward, the men quickly arrested the murderous foursome and bound them with heavy ropes.

Continuing through the hellish chambers, the armed men came upon still more dead girls all bearing the marks of torture. When they finally chanced upon the door of the countess's private chambers, even the most hardened among them hesitated. Then, making the sign of the cross as if to protect himself from the evil that waited within, Lord Thurzó stepped forward and kicked in the door.

Rising from an overstuffed chair, the richly clad visage of Countess Erzsébet Báthory came into view, cast by the hellish glow of the fireplace behind her. Momentarily startled by the intrusion, the aging countess, once famed for her haunting beauty, now stood amazed at the sight of the Palatine of Hungary himself standing in her chamber door with his sword drawn.

Twisting her face into an arrogant rage, the countess screamed, "How dare you enter my chambers in such a manner!"

Fueled by what he had seen that night, Thurzó grabbed the countess by the hair and dragged her out into the hallway kicking and screaming. Pulling her up short with a hard yank, Thurzó looked into her cold, hate-filled eyes and from behind clenched teeth exclaimed, "Madam, in the name of the king, you are under arrest."

If not for the arrest of the Countess Erzsébet Báthory that fateful night of December 29, 1610, the world may never have known of the extraordinary crimes committed by what is perhaps one of history's most prolific female serial killers. Báthory was accused of the torture and murder of as many as six hundred young girls during her life, and later historians alleged that she also practiced black magic against her political enemies, engaged in lesbian activities with her aunt, and worst of all, drank and bathed in the blood of her victims.

Born on August 7, 1560, at Ecsed Castle in what is now the eastern part of Hungary, Erzsébet Báthory was a precocious child known for uncontrollable fits of rage and violent seizures. Brought up in the privilege and wealth of an influential family of Hungarian nobles, she enjoyed all of the advantages her station afforded, including the best tutors in Eastern Europe and a small company of obedient servants who catered to her every whim.

By the age of fifteen Báthory was wed to an older man named Count Ferenc Nadasdy in a union that promised mutual advantage to both families. Nadasdy was a national hero to the Hungarian people through service against the Turks, but as captain of the Hungarian army he was also an absent husband. During what became known as the Fifteen Years' War, from 1593 to 1606, Nadasdy is listed as participating in every battle until his death on January 4, 1604, possibly from appendicitis. Besides his reputation as a Hungarian patriot, Ferenc Nadasdy was also known as a cruel and vicious opponent whom the Turks called "The Black Knight of Hungary." One report even mentions that Nadasdy reveled in entertaining his fellow knights by mockingly dancing with the corpses of his enemies or playing catch and kickball with the heads of executed prisoners.

Many historians believe that it was the bloodthirsty Nadasdy who first introduced the countess to the finer arts of torture during the brief periods when he was home. The two often severely punished their household servants for even the smallest infractions. One penalty Nadasdy particularly relished was to strip an offending servant girl of her clothes, cover her in honey, and force her to stand in the hot summer sun to be tormented by insects. Another favorite punishment was to insert pieces of oiled paper between the toes of servants who had passed out from overwork and light the pieces of paper on fire.

In this manner the couple reigned over their servants with terror and violence, and some have surmised that the young countess may even have periodically suffered the same treatment at the hands of her brutal husband when she did not comply with his wishes. Regardless of where Báthory first developed her taste for cruelty, her husband also acted to restrain her sadism from resulting in murder. For the "Hero of Hungary," murder brought suspicion and unwanted scrutiny, and in numerous recorded instances he hurried home from the front to cajole local officials into turning a blind eye to his wife's savage excesses.

With the death of her husband in 1604, however, there was suddenly nothing standing in the way of the countess, and it was from this period on that she developed her legendary taste for blood. Perhaps of one of the best known claims against the countess is that she regularly bathed in the blood of adolescent girls, whom she tortured and killed in the belief that their virginal blood would forever keep her young and beautiful. She is said to have stumbled upon the practice after striking a servant girl one day for some minor infraction. As the countess was wiping the servant's blood from her face and hands, she noticed that it left her skin looking fresher and rosier. Following the recommendation of a local witch named Anna Darvolya, whom she befriended, the countess immediately had the girl killed and drained of her blood, in which the countess bathed. The horrid act soon became a routine that she regularly performed with the aid of Darvolya in the dark hours of the night deep within her protective castle. Over time the countess enlisted the aid of four others to help her lure, with the promise of employment, local village girls to her castle, where they were tortured and killed. The first helper was a deformed boy named Janos Ujvary; the next was an old washer woman named Katalin Beneczky; and the final two were old servants named Ilona Jo Nagy and Dorottya Szentes.

Like her husband, the countess also had favorite forms of torture she indulged in, one of which included stripping a girl of her clothes and forcing her to stand in the freezing cold until she died of exposure. If the process seemed to be taking too long, she would douse her victim with buckets of cold water to speed things up. In other cases she stuck pins under the nails of some girls and cut their fingers off if they dared to try and remove the pins. Some she starved to death, others she cut or strangled, and many were beaten with an iron bar until they died from their wounds. When she was too weak or sick to do the job herself, she had the servants brought to her in bed, where she bit them viciously about the face and shoulders.

Many of the crimes the countess and her accomplices committed took place at Csejthe Castle, which she used as her base of power. Witnesses to many of the events testified afterwards that the countess maintained a series of inner rooms deep within the fortress that she kept under lock and guard and from which late at night the sounds of screams could be heard. When the bodies of her victims began piling up, disposing of them posed a major problem. At first they were secretly buried in the local cemetery at night, but as the cemetery filled up, Báthory's accomplices began stacking the bodies in the closets and under the beds of the castle. When her conspirators grew too lazy, they brazenly flung bodies over the battlements to be devoured by wolves.

As the years passed and the countess's deeds continued to go unpunished, she grew bold enough to make the one mistake that would bring her under the scrutiny of the royal court. Until now the countess had chosen her victims from the common peasant stock that resided within her holdings. Having depleted that source, she turned to young girls of noble families, whom she lured into her service with promises of advancement through the ranks of society.

When these girls started disappearing, the ruler of Hungary, King Matthias, began keeping an eye on the countess and her activities. The Hungarian court was after all indebted to the Báthory family for an extraordinary sum of money, which it had previously borrowed to help finance its wars against the Turks. If the countess were to be found guilty of some crime, then not only could the debt be erased but the king might have a claim to her vast estates. With continued complaints filtering in to the king from worried nobles over the mysterious deaths of their daughters, the court ordered the Lord Palatine (a high-level official) Count György Thurzó, coincidentally Báthory's own cousin, to arrest her in 1610.

On January 2, 1611, a trial ensued against the countess's four accomplices, who, after being tortured, confessed their crimes as well as the complicity of the countess herself. The four were quickly found guilty and sentenced to public execution while the countess, who was never officially tried, was sentenced to *perpetuis carceribus*, or perpetual life imprisonment. The punishment was meted out by bricking her in the tower room of her castle with only a small space to allow food to be passed inside. Three years into her sentence, on August 21, 1614, the countess was found dead of natural causes at the then ripe old age of fifty-four.

Despite her many protests of innocence there were few who believed her and even fewer who would support her against the crown. While the king failed to seize her lands, in the end he did manage to wipe out the sizable debt he owed. While the final body count was said to number as many as 650 young girls, this figure had one source: an unknown servant girl who based her claims on hearsay. More realistic estimates report that over the course of two decades it was probably closer to fifty. While none of the three hundred witnesses who gave testimony to her crimes actually saw her commit them with their own eyes, the accusations alone were enough to condemn her.

Indeed, legends of her bloody bathing rituals did not even surface until a hundred years after her death, when a Jesuit priest named László Turóczi collected stories from the villages surrounding Csejthe Castle during the height of the vampire mania that swept Eastern Europe in the 1700s. Though Erzsébet Báthory failed to find the immortality legend claims she sought in the blood of others, she may have finally achieved it in the gruesome legacy she left behind.

BLUEBEARD

… Lord de Rais and his followers, his accomplices, conveyed away a certain number of small children, or other persons, and had them snatched, whom they struck down and killed, to have their blood, heart, liver, or other such parts, to make them a sacrifice to the devil, or to do other sorceries with, on which subject there are numerous complaints.

—GEORGES BATAILLE, *THE TRIAL OF GILLES DE RAIS*

Once upon a time, in the Duchy of Brittany, there lived a wealthy and powerful nobleman known as Bluebeard, because he sported a large blue beard that lent him a rather frightening appearance. One day Bluebeard desired the young daughter of a neighboring lord, and after a period of courtship convinced her to marry him despite his fearsome countenance and the fact that his previous wives had all disappeared mysteriously.

As soon as the two were wed, they settled down in one of Bluebeard's many fine castles and lived peacefully until one day he abruptly told his new wife that he must leave on a long journey immediately. Saddling his steed in haste, Bluebeard turned and handed his wife a heavy ring of keys, stating, "On this ring are the keys that unlock every door within this great castle. As my wife you are free to roam about its halls and chambers as you see fit, but the small room deep within the castle's keep you must never enter, for the day you do you shall feel the wrath of my deadly anger." Taken aback by the fiery look in her husband's eyes, the young wife dutifully agreed to his command and waved goodbye as he spurred his horse through the postern gate.

Days went by, turning into weeks, as the young wife filled her time waiting for her husband to return by exploring the many twisting corridors and lofty staircases of the castle's interior. In time, however, she grew bored with these and found herself returning again and again to the very door that Bluebeard had forbidden her to enter. Finally one day her curiosity got the best of her, and wondering what great mysteries lay within, she slipped a key inside the door's worn lock face and heaved it open.

Adjusting her eyes to the stygian darkness, the young wife gasped in horror at the charnel house she beheld. From floor to ceiling the room was splashed in putrid-smelling blood as the badly mutilated bodies of Bluebeard's former wives hung from the walls like gruesome trophies. Reeling from the shock of it, the wife slammed the door shut remembering the words her husband spoke to her before leaving: *But the small room deep within the castle's keep you must never enter, for the day you do you shall feel the wrath of my deadly anger.*

That same evening Bluebeard unexpectedly returned from his travels, and after washing the dust from his massive blue beard demanded that his wife return the keys he had left in her safekeeping. Noticing how she trembled before him, Bluebeard's eyes narrowed into angry slits as he hissed, "So, now you know my secret, do you not, my love?"

Falling to her knees, the frightened wife cried out, "Please, my lord, I did not mean to disobey your wishes."

But Bluebeard's cold heart would show no pity. As he slowly drew his sword, he exclaimed, "Now, good wife, you will finally join my other wives and make a fine addition to my wall."

Before Bluebeard could deliver the deadly blow, however, a loud crash sounded at the chamber door, and in burst the wife's two brothers with their swords drawn—she having sent word to her family of the danger she was in. In order to save himself, Bluebeard turned to run, but the brothers were quicker and ran him through with their blades, ending his life and saving their sister from the horrifying fate that awaited her in that bloody room deep within the confines of the castle's keep.

The bloody tale of Bluebeard was known to exist long before Charles Perrault first published it in his 1697 collection of French folktales entitled *Histoires ou contes du temps passé*. Some even speculate that it was created as a veiled warning by the peasantry of Brittany to caution children to steer clear of real-life Bluebeards and their castles in a time when accusing the French nobility of any crime could mean the loss of one's own head.

Who, then, was this French nobleman who so terrorized the countryside of Brittany to the extent that he was immortalized in the folktales of the French people? While several candidates have been put forward by scholars over the years, many attribute the origin of the tale to one of the country's greatest knights, Gilles de Rais, who fought his way through the ranks to become Marshal of France.

He was born in 1404 to Guy de Laval-Montmorency and Marie de Craon at the family's castle at Machecoul. Both his parents died while Gilles was still very young, and he afterwards found himself under the tutelage of his scheming grandfather, Jean de Craon. Left to his own devices as a child, few if any restraints were placed upon him—and while some education was afforded him, most of his time was spent preparing for his introduction to the battlefields of France. During the frequent and violent clashes that later became known as the Hundred Years' War, Gilles distinguished himself as a courageous and reckless warrior earning many honors upon the field. In 1420, Gilles inherited his father's estates and increased his fortune by marrying Catherine de Thouars.

For a French nobleman of the period, however, the only true profession was that of war, and from 1427 to 1435 he served as a commander in the royal army, fighting alongside Joan of Arc against the English and their Burgundian allies. After the siege of Orléans in 1429, Gilles and three other lords were rewarded with the honor of transporting the holy oil of Saint Remy to Notre-Dame de Reims for the coronation of Charles VII as King of France, after which Gilles was named Marshal of France.

A few years after Joan of Arc was burned at the stake as a witch by her English enemies in 1431, Gilles hung up his spurs and sword and retired to his vast estates, where he quickly squandered his wealth with extravagant displays and costly theatrical productions. Before long these excesses threatened to bankrupt him, and he did the unthinkable for a French nobleman: he began selling off his holdings to pay for his uncontrolled spending. Feeling the pinch, Gilles also looked for alternative solutions to his dwindling funds and several times found himself swindled by charlatans claiming to be magicians who could turn base metals into gold through alchemy. When these failed, Gilles grew more desperate and began experimenting with the occult under the direction of an equally suspicious character named Francesco Prelati, who claimed to be able to raise a demon he called by the name "Baron." It was this demon, Gilles later testified, that first provided the impetus for his ghastly crimes, as Prelati promised the restoration of his fortune if he would but sacrifice the lives of innocent children to the evil fiend.

Regardless of whether Gilles truly believed that torturing and murdering children would satisfy the demon Baron or, as is more likely the case, he was simply satisfying his own inner demons, it's believed that he began his bloody work in the spring of 1432 after the death of his grandfather. Most of the abductions involved local village children whose parents were powerless to complain and occurred deep inside the moated walls of his castle at Machecoul, where even their screams could not be heard. The first documented case concerned a twelve-year-old boy named Jeudon, an apprentice furrier. Gilles's cousins, Gilles de Sille and Roger de Briqueville, asked the boy to deliver a message to the castle, but when he failed to return the accomplices told inquirers that the boy must have been carried off by bandits.

Often the crimes followed a ritualistic pattern. They began subtly with a twisted game of cat and mouse that involved dressing the abducted child in fine clothes and setting before him a feast unlike anything he had seen before. As the child ate with relish, Gilles and a small band of confidants riotously feasted and drank a mixture of heated spice wine known as hippocras. Then when the party reached a fever pitch, the child was suddenly taken to a private room where Gilles had him strung up with ropes and strangled while he watched. Many tortures and abuses were committed against his victims before they were finally beheaded with a thick, double-edged blade known as a braquemard. Witnesses to these horrific events later reported that Gilles also stabbed some in the jugular and allowed the warm blood to cover him, which he drank with great excitement. When the men were done with the victim, the body and any traces of the crime were destroyed by fire and the ashes dumped into the castle's moat.

Such atrocities might have gone unpunished if Gilles's own greed and arrogance had not gotten the better of him. On May 15, 1440, he and a small band of armed followers kidnapped a local cleric during a dispute over property Gilles had sold to the clergyman's brother and now intended to take back by force. The incident prompted an investigation by the Bishop of Nantes, who in the process uncovered shocking evidence of Gilles's darker crimes. In short order, Gilles and two close servants, Henriet and Poitou, were arrested and charged with unspeakable crimes ranging from witchcraft to murder. During the trial that followed, Gilles did little to exonerate himself in the eyes of the court but to the contrary exhibited a number of bizarre behaviors, including attempts at bribing the court and delusions that he was a Carmelite monk. In the end, however, Gilles finally admitted to the charges against him in all the graphic details he could muster for the court scribes who took his confession. He was condemned to die by the hangman's noose.

At nine o'clock on October 26, 1440, Gilles and his co-defendants were led to their place of execution on the Île de Nantes, where in a crowded meadow he addressed onlookers with contrition and remorse, even extolling Henriet and Poitou to die bravely and think of salvation. Gilles was then hung by the neck until dead, after which the body was carried away to an unknown resting place. His co-defendants also faced the rope, and afterwards, like many of their young victims, were burned to ashes and scattered to the wind.

It's difficult to truly account for the number of children who fell into the clutches of the bloodthirsty Gilles de Rais, since he carefully disposed of the bodies. Most of his victims, both boys and girls, ranged in age between six and eighteen, and while some historians claim the final body count is somewhere between eighty and two hundred, others have estimated it could be as high as six hundred.

Although Gilles de Rais achieved many triumphs on the battlefield in defense of his country, it will be his crimes history remembers most. Several years after his execution, his daughter Marie erected a stone memorial at the place of his execution, which over generations became strangely regarded as a holy altar until it was destroyed by Jacobins during the French Revolution. Now all that remains of Gilles de Rais are horror stories told to children to keep them awake at night.

Count Dracula: Without me, Transylvania will be as exciting
as Bucharest … on a Monday night.

—LOVE AT FIRST BITE

6

A S+AR IS B⊕RN

The concept of a supernatural creature that preyed upon the blood of humans left an indelible mark on the accounts that survived the rise and fall of early civilizations. From the Babylonian *Epic of Gilgamesh* sprang vengeful ghosts and demons; in the Sanskrit *Bhagavad Gita*, blood-drinking gods battled one another atop fields of corpses; and from the weathered scrolls of the Greeks, seductive *lamia* led unwary young men to their end. Regardless of which dark shape the vampire took, such tales continued to trickle down through the stream of human consciousness as a literary theme to explain some of humanity's deepest fears.

Nevertheless, for much of the vampire's history it remained a secondary character when compared to the shining gods and heroes that populated the vast majority of early mythologies. Ironically, the theme didn't step forward as a distinct literary device of its own until the Age of Enlightenment dawned across Europe in the 1700s, when many great thinkers were turning away from the mysticism and superstition of the past in favor of science and reason. Sparked by extraordinary reports of vampirism in Eastern Europe, such as the cases of Arnod Paole and Peter Plogojowitz, churchmen, scientists, and political leaders alike wrote and debated prolifically on the subject, lending credibility to vampires far beyond their folkloric roots.

For the next one hundred years, intellectual works were circulated to the public in the form of pamphlets, treatises, and books at an ever-increasing pace. In 1732, for example, as many as fourteen works on vampirism appeared in German-speaking lands alone, while each day newspapers across Europe reported new outbreaks. With this rise in media attention, or because of it, reports poured in at an alarming rate, with cases popping up in Prussia in 1710, 1721, and 1750; in Hungary from 1725 to 1730; in Bulgaria in 1775; in Wallachia in 1756; and in Russia in 1772. In each case, newspapers vied with one another in the race to see who could capture the most graphic details or report the highest body count, lending to each new story a greater element of sensationalism. Yet as much as readers feared the very mention of the word *vampire*, they were equally enthralled by it and hungered for more.

LITERARY VAMPIRES

One of the earliest appearances of a vampire in a fictional work of literature was in a short poem published by the German writer Heinrich August Ossenfelder in 1748, entitled "Der Vampir." In the poem a man threatens to drink the blood of a young Christian maiden if she spurns his attentions, and by doing so acts as a metaphor for those forces menacing the Christian church during that period. Other works followed, including, in 1797, Johann Wolfgang von Goethe's poem "The Bride of Corinth," which explored similar themes *sans* the blood drinking, as well as Robert Southey's 1801 *Thalaba the Destroyer*, which is the first piece of English fiction to mention vampires. The theme wouldn't truly come into its own though until 1813, when the British poet Lord Byron published a poem entitled "The Giaour," describing a corpse-like revenant that prowls abandoned tombs at night in search of blood. A portion of the poem reads:

> But first, on earth as Vampire sent,
> Thy corse shall from its tomb be rent:
> Then ghastly haunt thy native place,
> And suck the blood of all thy race:
> There from thy daughter, sister, wife,
> At midnight drain the stream of life;
> Yet loathe the banquet which perforce
> Must feed thy livid living corse ...
> Wet with thine own blest blood shall drip
> Thy gnashing tooth and haggard lip;
> Then stalking to thy sullen grave
> Go—and with the Ghouls and Afrits rave;
> Till these in horror shrink away
> From spectre more accursed than they!

Lord Byron based the work on tales he heard while traveling through Eastern Europe, specifically during his stay at the court of Ali Pasha in Albania, and the poem went on to meet with widespread acclaim from both critics and readers alike.

While many of these earlier works still relied on the folkloric imagery of a monster running amuck in the graveyard at night, an important paradigm shift began to take place in how writers and therefore readers saw the vampire. On April Fool's Day 1819, a groundbreaking new short story entitled "The Vampyre" appeared in the English journal *New Monthly Magazine*. Penned by none other than Lord Byron's former physician John William Polidori, the inspiration for the tale began as all good horror stories do: on a dark and stormy night.

Byron and Polidori were staying at the Villa Diodati near the shores of Lake Geneva, in Switzerland, in the summer of 1816 with the poet Percy Shelley; his soon-to-be wife, Mary Godwin; and Godwin's stepsister, Claire Clairmont. Inclement weather kept the small group confined indoors most days, but at night they amused themselves by reading horror stories to one another. On one such night, as the rain pelted the shutters and lightning flashed outside, someone proposed they have a contest to see who could write the best ghost story. The result of the challenge produced two of the greatest works in horror literature to date: Mary Shelley's *Frankenstein, or The Modern Prometheus* and Polidori's "The Vampyre."

In Polodori's vampire tale, a young Englishman named Aubrey meets the mysterious aristocrat Lord Ruthven. While the two are traveling across Europe together, they are set upon by a ruthless gang of bandits, resulting in Lord Ruthven receiving a mortal wound. Before succumbing to his injuries, he makes Aubrey swear an oath upon his honor to keep his death a secret from the world for one year and one day. Aubrey soon after returns home to England, where he is shocked to find Lord Ruthven very much alive and well, and although he suspects a supernatural influence at work he is honor-bound to keep the secret. Aubrey's horror is further compounded when he learns that his sister and Lord Ruthven are engaged to be married on the very day his oath is to expire. As the story climaxes, Aubrey writes a letter to his sister warning her of the danger she faces, but the correspondence arrives too late. Lord Ruthven has already married the young, unsuspecting girl and murdered her on their wedding day before disappearing into the night.

While "The Vampyre" became a bestseller across Europe, running through numerous editions and translations, many at the time attributed the work to Lord Byron, even as he emphatically denied it. The relationship between the two men quickly soured after their stay at the villa, and they went their separate ways never to speak again, but many scholars believe that Polidori based his vampire character on Lord Byron himself.

The genius of the work, however, lay not in the act of the author maligning his former employer, but in the way he turned the very idea of the vampire upside down. Polidori dragged the vampire from its dank tomb, dusted him off, gave him expensive clothes and a crisp new English accent, and set him loose to roam among the well-bred of society. With this new take on the old tale, John William Polidori in turn created a new vampire—the romantic vampire. Unfortunately for Polidori, however, he never realized the importance he played in the annuals of the vampire, as he committed suicide in London on August 24, 1821, by drinking cyanide.

Yet while the author may have perished, the legacy he helped to found lived on, and in 1845 the Scottish writer James Malcolm Rymer picked up the thread by releasing the gothic horror story *Varney the Vampire, or The Feast of Blood*. Appearing from 1845 to 1847 in serialized installments known as "penny dreadfuls" (because of their inexpensive cost and bloodcurdling storylines), the work when collected in its entirety spanned 850 pages over 220 chapters.

The series begins with a brutal vampire named Sir Francis Varney terrorizing a family, the Bannerworths. From there on the storyline, which is confusing enough, weaves its way in and out of various plot twists, barely keeping to its narrative. Characters come and go, and there are even hints that Varney is related to his victims; readers are told that he bears a strong resemblance to a portrait in Bannerworth Hall of the late Marmaduke Bannerworth.

Despite its ponderous and convoluted storyline, the uniqueness of the work lay in the evolution of its main character. In early installments Rymer portrayed Varney as a bloodthirsty and remorseless creature bent on revenge, yet as the tale progresses the vampire is seen with increasing sympathy as a man cursed for the ages with a condition he cannot escape. While Varney meets his end on a number of occasions, he is forced to rise each time to carry on the nightmare of his existence. His final end, and that of the series, comes when Varney casts himself into the fires of Mount Vesuvius, leaving a written account of his life with a priest.

Unlike Polidori's infamous Lord Ruthven, who struts across the pages as the quintessential aristocrat of polish and sophistication, Varney was written to be far more monstrous in both his appearance and his intentions. Rymer also employed many of the vampiric themes and conventions modern readers have come to recognize in the creature today, including supernatural strength, hypnotic powers, and fangs that left puncture marks in the necks of his victims. He did not, however, saddle his villain with some of the limitations associated with vampires, such as an aversion to sunlight, garlic, and religious icons.

In 1872, twenty-five years after Varney ceased to terrify readers, a novella entitled *Carmilla* appeared as a three-part series in the magazine *The Dark Blue*. Composed by Dublin-born mystery writer Sheridan Le Fanu, the story was later collected for publication in the book *In a Glass Darkly*, which featured a number of gothic and mystery tales by the author.

Narrated by the heroine Laura, the suspense-driven tale begins with a carriage accident near her family's castle in the forests of Styria that brings into her life a girl of the same age named Carmilla. While Carmilla is recuperating at the castle, her mother oddly announces that she must leave on pressing business and will return in three months' time to fetch her daughter. During Carmilla's stay, the two girls become fast friends, and while their relationship blossoms so do Carmilla's romantic advances towards Laura. Before long Laura grows suspicious of her new companion, who carefully avoids speaking of her past and prefers to sleep most of the day and roam about at night.

When a painting arrives at the castle of Laura's ancestor Mircalla, Countess of Karnstein, its resemblance to Carmilla is uncanny. Eventually Laura tracks down the grave of her ancestor Mircalla—only to be attacked by Carmilla, who finally reveals herself as a vampire. Soon the vampire hunter Baron

Vordenburg joins the cast and helps locate Carmilla's secret tomb, where an imperial commission is convened to exhume and destroy Carmilla's sleeping corpse.

With *Carmilla*, Le Fanu departed from the accepted role of the vampire as a primarily male seducer and also infused within the tale erotic undertones between the two main female characters that have labeled Carmilla one of the first lesbian vampires in the history of literature—although not the last. The name of Laura's ancestor Mircalla is of course an anagram for Carmilla, and thus once again highlights the familial aspect of the vampire to its victim present in so much folklore. Yet Le Fanu was also not above adding his own inventions to the mix. In the story, Carmilla slept in a coffin by day, exhibited an unnatural beauty, could pass through solid walls, and could assume the form of a fiendish-looking black cat when she so chose.

In 1897 another Irish author, Bram Stoker, built on the success of his predecessors and burst onto the literary scene with a sensational vampire novel entitled *Dracula*. First produced in a hardback edition on May 26, 1897, by the publisher Archibald Constable and Company, the novel lived on to give audiences its most enduring image of the vampire to date, spawning numerous other books, plays, and movies across genres as diverse as horror, science fiction, and even comedy. Stoker, who was the business manager for the world-famous Lyceum Theatre in London at the time, wrote the novel to supplement his income, originally calling it *The Dead Un-Dead* and then just *The Undead* before settling on the name of its main character, Dracula, for the title.

In the epistolary novel, told through a series of letters, journal entries, and even a ship's log, an English solicitor named Jonathan Harker travels to Count Dracula's castle in the wild Carpathian Mountains of Transylvania to finalize the purchase of certain properties. Once there he unwittingly becomes the prisoner of the count and for a time falls under the spell of three female vampires. With Harker trapped in the ancient castle, Dracula makes his way to England on the Russian ship the *Demeter*, which washes ashore along the northeastern English coast with all its crew either missing or dead. Now loose in the English countryside, Dracula begins to menace Harker's fiancée, Mina, and her friend Lucy. When Lucy falls ill with a strange wasting disease, Professor Abraham Van Helsing is called in to treat her, but despite his best efforts Lucy dies shortly after his arrival. Following her burial she begins to rise from the grave each night as one of the undead, forcing Van Helsing and several of her former friends to drive a stake through her heart and decapitate her.

While these events are transpiring, Harker escapes Dracula's castle and makes his way to Budapest, where Mina joins him and the two are married. The newlyweds return to England, where they join Van Helsing and others in the hunt for Count Dracula. In the process Mina is bitten by Dracula three times before he flees back to his native land of Transylvania. In hot pursuit the vampire hunters catch up with him just outside his castle walls as the sun begins to rise. In a final climactic scene, one of the vampire hunters slashes the throat of Dracula while another pierces his heart with a knife. Dracula then crumbles into dust as the sun crests the mountain's peaks. The puncture marks on Mina's neck disappear, signaling that she is free of the vampire's influence.

A major part of the novel's success lay in Stoker's spine-tingling depiction of Count Dracula, which relied on a blending of both the tragic Byronic figure popular with his Victorian audience and more primitive animalistic elements that added a heightened sense of horror to his character. Dracula could on the one hand appear a charming and cultured gentleman out for an evening at the opera, while at the same time he moved through the pages of the story like a wild beast, crawling down walls head first or commanding rats and wolves to his bidding. Yet Dracula was more than any of the vampire characters that came before him, and in a sense became the model by which later writers and moviemakers styled their vampires. He slept in coffins filled with the soil of his native land, avoided sunlight at all costs, drank the blood of beautiful women, commanded the weather, and avoided crucifixes whenever possible.

To help formulate his frightful masterpiece, Stoker drew heavily on earlier works, including Polidori's "The Vampyre" and Le Fanu's *Carmilla*. He also spent considerable effort researching Eastern European folklore and borrowed from sources such as Emily Gerard's 1885 essay "Transylvania Superstitions." To further flesh out his arch-villain, Stoker turned to William Wilkinson's 1820 *Account of the Principalities of Wallachia and Moldavia with Various Political Observations Relating to Them*, and there found mention of the infamous tyrant Dracula, to whom he forever linked his fictional character.

Despite the standing *Dracula* enjoys today, Stoker's novel was slow to catch on with Victorian readers, who passed the work off as just another gothic adventure novel and one of many "invasion" stories flooding the market that featured creatures or other supernatural forces invading the British

Isles. Even the sinister character of Count Dracula himself wouldn't gain iconic status until after Stoker's death, when the novel was adapted for the silver screen in 1931.

As time marched on and the prominence of the vampire genre grew, writers continued to transform the image and even the idea of the vampire in ways to meet the needs of each new generation of readers. While in most cases the vampire remained a bloodsucking monster that preyed upon humanity, writers in the mid-twentieth century departed from traditional storylines in order to shock their audiences in new and more interesting ways.

In 1954 Richard Matheson published the novel *I Am Legend*, which combined the horror of vampirism with the science of a post-apocalyptic world consumed by a deadly plague. The tale later inspired three separate movies: 1964's *The Last Man on Earth,* with Vincent Price; 1971's *The Omega Man,* starring Charlton Heston; and *I Am Legend*, the 2007 movie featuring Will Smith.

In 1976 Colin Wilson added yet another new spin to the old tale by casting his vampires as a race of wandering space aliens come to earth to drain humans of their life force, in the appropriately titled novel *The Space Vampires*. Then, in 1986, vampire fans were treated to another reworking when Brian Lumley created his fantastic *Necroscope* series, in which vampiric parasites known as the Wamphyri spill into our world from another universe.

Yet as far-reaching and imaginative as these other works are, one of the most influential vampire tales since *Dracula* is Anne Rice's *Interview with the Vampire*, first published in 1976. The novel opens in the New Orleans of the late 1700s, and the story is told from the perspective of the vampire Louis, who is cursed to become a blood drinker after being bitten by a vampire named Lestat. Throughout the early portions of the novel, the two vampires are close accomplices as Louis struggles with his new life as one of the undead. Lestat creates another vampire to add to their cozy little "family," a small girl named Claudia, but further divisions arise in their relationship that threaten to tear them apart.

Eventually things come to a head when Claudia poisons Lestat, slits his throat, and dumps the body in the swamps outside the city. Louis and Claudia then flee to Europe in search of other vampires like themselves, and in time encounter the vampire Armand and his coven, the Théâtre des Vampires in Paris. Before long the two new arrivals are accused of trying to kill their maker when Lestat reappears, having survived Claudia's assassination attempt, and charges them with the crime. As punishment Louis is locked in a coffin to starve to death while Claudia is exposed to sunlight and killed. Armand then releases Louis, who in revenge destroys the coven, and the two set off for America together.

After the release of *Interview with the Vampire*, additional novels followed, many furthering the tale of the vampire Lestat, which became collectively known as the *The Vampire Chronicles*. What set Rice's vampires apart from their predecessors was their internal struggles with the guilt and loneliness that consumed their cursed state. In this regard, Rice's vampires became more human than any who came before and set the trend for future books and movies, which portrayed the creatures as tragically romantic figures at odds with themselves and the world around them. Based on the success of Rice's vampire books, in 1994 a film adapta-

tion of *Interview with the Vampire* appeared, starring Brad
Pitt, Antonio Banderas, Christian Slater, and Tom Cruise.

CEN+ER S+AGE

About the time that vampires were finding a new lease on
life in the works of nineteenth-century writers, they began
making an appearance on the stage as well. Inspired by Polidori's story "The Vampyre," a theatrical production entitled
Le Vampire was first adapted for the Paris stage on June 13,
1820, by the French author Charles Nodier, who took the lib-
erty when revising Polidori's work to relocate the storyline
to Scotland. A few months later, the British dramatist James
Planché introduced *The Vampire, or The Bride of the Isles* to the
world at the Lyceum Theatre in London, on August 9, 1820.
This production was one of the first to feature the special effect known as the "vampire trap," in which a trap door in the
stage floor or wall quickly opened and shut, allowing the
actor to appear or disappear as if by magic. Nodier's earlier
work also inspired the two-act German opera *Der Vampyr* by
composer Heinrich Marschner, which was first performed in
Leipzig on March 29, 1828, and met with instant success.
Even Alexandre Dumas, the author of such works as *The
Three Musketeers* and *The Count of Monte Cristo*, got in on the
action with a production similarly titled *Le Vampire* in 1851.

Perhaps one of the more interesting venues in which such
dramas appeared was the infamous Le Théâtre du Grand-
Guignol, which literally means "The Theatre of the Big Puppet." First opening in Paris in 1897, the theater was located
within a former church and lured in Parisian audiences with
horror plays featuring particularly gory special effects and

bloody climaxes. For over sixty years the theater thrilled audiences, until it was forced to close in 1962 when it found modern theatergoers too desensitized by the horrors of two world wars to be captivated by its performances any longer.

Even the legendary *Dracula* was originally intended to be adapted for the stage by its author, Bram Stoker, who held readings of the work before its publication in the hopes of attracting interest in it as a drama. Unfortunately for Stoker, he never did get a theatrical version off the ground, but more than a decade after his death an actor named Hamilton Deane and a journalist named John Balderston produced it for the stage featuring a little-known Hungarian actor named Bela Lugosi in the title role. From the moment it first appeared on Broadway in 1927, American audiences flocked to its performances, which were craftily advertised to theatergoers, informing them that "... it would be wise for them to visit a specialist and have their hearts examined before subjecting them to the fearful thrills and shocks that Dracula had in store for them" (Deane 1960, 107–8).

LIGH+S, CAℿERA, FANGS

On March 15, 1922, a grainy, black-and-white silent film premiered at Berlin's Kino Primus-Palast under the eerie title *Nosferatu, eine Symphonie des Grauens*, or *Nosferatu: A Symphony of Horror*. A product of the German Expressionist F. W. Murnau, the movie follows a man named Thomas Hutter, who is sent to Transylvania by his employer to visit the mysterious Count Orlok at his castle in the mountains. Once he arrives, Hutter discovers the count is a vampire, and after wandering through the castle finds Orlok lying in a coffin in the castle crypt. Hutter flees the castle and makes his way back to his wife in Germany, where unbeknownst to him Orlok takes up residence as well. Ellen, Hutter's wife, eventually stumbles across a book in her husband's possession titled *The Book of Vampires*, from which she learns that to kill a vampire a woman pure of heart must let him drink her blood until he forgets how much time has passed and the sun comes up to destroy him. During this time a number of grisly murders take place in the town, but the townsfolk merely think some strange disease is plaguing their homes. Then one night Count Orlok enters Ellen's bedchamber and begins to drink her blood, but just as stated in *The Book of Vampires*, because she is pure at heart the monster forgets to flee before the sun comes up, and as the cock crows he vanishes into smoke for good.

While the numerous similarities between the film *Nosferatu* and the novel *Dracula* are hard to miss, Murnau did make some departures from the stereotypical vampire and portrayed Count Orlok as a monster with ratlike ears, a gaunt demonic face, and long taloned fingernails resembling claws. Also of importance is that Orlok's bite does not create other vampires as Stoker's Dracula did. Instead, Orlok's victims die from what the townspeople believe is the plague, appealing to the traditional German belief that vampires were carriers of unknown contagions. Despite these disparities, however, it was apparent to most that *Nosferatu* was little more than a thinly veiled copy of *Dracula*. More importantly, it was readily apparent to Stoker's widow, Florence, who sued Murnau for plagiarism and copyright infringement.

After rulings in her favor both in 1924 and 1929, the film was ordered to be destroyed, but because so many copies had already been released for distribution, it became impossible to round them all up. As a result, copies of the terrifying film entered general circulation anyway and over the years garnered a loyal cult following with horror film aficionados and movie historians to this very day.

Even though Murnau's silent Count Orlok definitely raised the bar on creepiness, arguably the most well-known vampire film of the twentieth century is Tod Browning's 1931 version of *Dracula*. Optioned by Universal Pictures from Florence Stoker for the sum of $40,000, the movie script closely followed Deane and Balderston's popular Broadway version just as it in turn mirrored the original novel. Although the film stared the Hungarian-born actor Bela Lugosi, who was the lead in the Broadway version as well, he was not the studio's first choice and only won the role after Browning's first pick, Lon Chaney, Sr., died of lung cancer in 1930.

When the film premiered at the lavish Roxy Theatre in New York on February 12, 1931, executives at Universal Pictures had no idea what to expect, but from the first moment the lights dimmed audiences were awestruck. As the show opened in other theaters across the country, movie houses were forced to offer round-the-clock screenings just to accommodate the demand. Industry figures claim that in its first domestic release it earned $700,000 with sales of $1.2 million worldwide (Guiley 2005, 109).

While there are many who claim the film's success can be attributed to the chilling performance of Bela Lugosi, the actor himself was only paid $500 a week for his role and was forced to declare bankruptcy one year after the movie was released. While Lugosi went on to star in other horror films with little success, he will always be remembered for his iconic portrayal of Count Dracula, and when he died in 1956 he was buried in the vampire cape he wore during the film's shooting.

Given *Dracula*'s success, Universal Pictures continued to crank out sequels to the film, including *Dracula's Daughter* in 1936, *Son of Dracula* in 1943, and *House of Dracula* in 1945. By the 1950s, the British company Hammer Films began producing vampire films in color, often starring Christopher Lee as a much more calculatingly evil Dracula and Peter Cushing as his vampire-hunting nemesis. These began a new slew of vampire movies that lasted until the 1970s and included such films as *The Brides of Dracula* in 1960, *The Satanic Rites of Dracula* in 1973, and the ever-campy kung-fu flick *The Legend of the 7 Golden Vampires* in 1974.

On June 27, 1966, teenagers across the country began arriving home just in time to catch the new gothic soap opera *Dark Shadows*, which aired on the ABC network each weekday at 4 PM for one half-hour. Created by director and producer Dan Curtis, who claimed to have been inspired by a dream he had of a girl taking a long train ride to a large dark mansion, the production spanned 1,225 episodes from 1966 to 1971, and at its peak claimed over eighteen million viewers. Starting in black and white, the show made the transition to color in 1967 and was comprised of a relatively small cast of characters who played many parts.

While *Dark Shadows* did not at first include a supernatural element in its storyline, it introduced a vampire character into the mix in the hopes of boosting sagging ratings one year into its run. When the 175-year-old vampire Barnabas Collins, played by Jonathan Frid, finally made his daytime debut, the show soared to new heights—until April 2, 1971, by which time a sharp rise in competing soaps and a decline in television advertising condemned *Dark Shadows* to the chopping block.

In the series, a charismatic vampire named Barnabas Collins makes his entrance after being locked away in a sarcophagus on the Collinwood Estate for many years. Once he is accidentally freed by a Collins family servant who was in search of buried jewels, Barnabas masquerades as a distant family relative from England and insidiously works his way into the family's good graces. From there the storyline twists and weaves its way into fantastic plotlines that combine time travel, ghosts, Dr. Jekyll and Mr. Hyde, witches, werewolves, and sinister cults. Throughout all of this, Barnabas falls in love, is cured of his vampirism, and in time is cursed to it again.

Like the similar tale of *Varney the Vampire* over one hundred years before him, Barnabas finds his character transforming over the course of the series from a run-of-the-mill bloodsucker to a star-crossed figure desperate for a cure to the curse that afflicts him. In 1991 NBC attempted to revive the series with a remake, but after only twelve episodes the show lost momentum and was canceled. Even now, at the time of the writing of this book, a film version of *Dark Shadows* is slated for release in 2012, directed by Tim Burton and starring Johnny Depp and Michelle Pfeiffer.

As serious traditional vampire dramas such as *Dark Shadows* were fizzling out on TV, lighter versions such as producer Joss Whedon's *Buffy the Vampire Slayer* were proving that viewers were still in love with the concept. Airing from March 10, 1997, until May 20, 2003, the show ran successfully for seven seasons with three Emmys and numerous other awards under its belt. Broadly based on Whedon's campy 1992 movie of the same name, the weekly series followed the exploits of Buffy

Summers, played by Sarah Michelle Gellar, as she battled vampires, demons, and a host of other dark minions all the while attending Sunnydale High School. Aiding her quest are an assortment of teenage friends and a Watcher, who guides and teaches the group—who call themselves the "Scooby Gang"—in the subtle art of killing vampires. Given the show's trendiness, humor, and contemporary teenage themes, it was immensely popular and produced a host of spinoff books, comics, action figures, games, and even a second series titled *Angel*, making up what many fans and even some academic scholars have come to call the "Buffyverse."

The times, it seemed, were again a-changing, and so too was the public's perception of the vampire motif in popular culture. Vampires were once seen by illiterate European peasants as bloated corpses feeding on the blood of the living, but modern audiences craved more from their monsters and demanded that their vampires become the heroes or even the love interests of the story. One case in point was the 1998 film *Blade*, which featured a vampire hunter by the same name, played by Wesley Snipes, who not only hunts down vampires with a vengeance but is part vampire himself. Based on a 1970s Marvel comic book character that first appeared in *The Tomb of Dracula*, this gun-toting, sword-welding superhero went on to appear in several sequels to the franchise, as well as in a television series in 2006.

Another example is the 2003 action-adventure film *Underworld*, in which bands of leather-clad vampires face off against packs of howling werewolves in a blood feud lasting centuries. The main character, a vampire named Selene, played by Kate Beckinsale, falls in love with a human and must in the end protect him from both sides in a sort of machine gun–blazing undead version of *Romeo and Juliet*.

The final and probably the most potent manifestation of this new obsession with vampires is the *Twilight Saga*, which includes the 2008 teenage vampire romance film *Twilight*, adapted from the popular novel by author Stephenie Meyer. In the film Isabella "Bella" Swan, played by Kristen Stewart, moves to the small town of Forks, Washington, where she falls in with Edward Cullen, a 104-year-old vampire who only drinks animal blood. Eventually another vampire named James arrives and tries to kill Bella for sport, but Edward intervenes and in a climactic battle kills James.

While critics gave the film mixed reviews, teenagers and even some adults went wild over the movie, which grossed an amazing $392 million worldwide, as well as spawning fan clubs, movie merchandise, and several sequels also based on Meyer's novels, including *New Moon* in 2009, *Eclipse* in 2010, and *Breaking Dawn, Part 1* in 2011. (*Breaking Dawn, Part 2*, the final movie in the *Twilight Saga* series, will be released in late 2012.)

By examining these and other works, we can find, within human history, literature, and even within the still relatively new medium of film, the ever-changing progression of humanity's view of the vampire. Yet not until the Victorian period of the 1800s did writers create the truly powerful and seductive blood drinkers we know and love today. From bloodthirsty menace to superhero and lover, the vampire has come a long way in the imagination of the public. But as is often the case, truth can be stranger than fiction, and as we will see in the next few chapters, real vampires are often much different from the ones we dream up.

Listen to them ... children of the night. What music they make!

—*DRACULA*, 1931

7

CHILDREN
⊕F +HE NIGH+

On November 25, 1996, the bludgeoned bodies of forty-nine-year-old Richard Wendorf and his wife, Ruth, age fifty-four, were discovered in their rural home in East Eustis, Florida. Police officials arriving on the scene speculated that intruders must have entered the home through an attached garage, and after stumbling upon Mr. Wendorf dozing on the couch, beat him to death with a blunt object. Mrs. Wendorf, upon hearing the commotion, rushed to her husband's aid and was in turn killed with the same murder weapon. Panicking, the intruders then fled, taking the couple's credit cards and their 1994 Ford Explorer.

Yet despite the obvious *modus operandi* of the murderers, two key facts lent the crime a sinister aspect: the first was a cryptic letter *V* burned onto the chest of Mr. Wendorf with a cigarette, and the second was that the Wendorf's teenage daughter Heather was missing.

Four days later and over six hundred miles across the country, five disheveled teenagers, including Heather Wendorf, were apprehended in Baton Rouge, Louisiana, driving the Wendorfs' stolen Explorer. The arrest made headlines across the nation, and not for obvious reasons such as the youth of the offenders or the heinousness of their crime, but for the startling claim they made to authorities that they were a clan of modern vampires. During the investigation that followed, sixteen-year-old Rod Ferrell, the self-proclaimed leader of the "clan," claimed that he was a five-hundred-year-old vampire with no soul, who preferred to be known by his vampire name "Vasego." While he initially blamed the murders on a rival vampire group, he soon changed his story and confessed to beating the Wendorfs to death with a crowbar he found in their garage. Following the murder, he and another clan member named Scott Anderson burned the *V* into Mr. Wendorf's chest as a sort of macabre calling card.

Days before the murders, the teenagers had left their homes in Murray, Kentucky, and drove to Eustis, Florida, at the behest of the Wendorf's daughter Heather, who planned to run away with the group to New Orleans. Heather had been friends with Ferrell years before, when he lived in Eustis for a short time with his mother. After he moved to Murray, the two remained in touch, during which time, according to Ferrell, Heather constantly complained that her parents were abusive. When the teens arrived, Heather joined several of the female members at a nearby cemetery for a blood-drinking initiation ritual while Ferrell and Anderson went to her home to collect her things. Once there, Ferrell made up his mind to murder the Wendorfs in their home and leave his vampire mark on the body of Mr. Wendorf. Heather would later testify that she did not know of Ferrell's murderous intentions that night and that afterwards she was terrified to leave the group, fearing she would be their next victim.

On February 12, 1998, Ferrell pleaded guilty to the premeditated murders of Richard and Ruth Wendorf and was sentenced to death in the Florida state prison electric chair, making him the youngest inmate on death row until his sentence was later commuted to life without parole. Scott Anderson, his accomplice, was sentenced to life without parole, while the remaining teenagers received sentences of up to ten years. The only exception was Heather Wendorf, who was never charged in the case and who went on to cooperate with author Aphrodite Jones on her book, *The Embrace: A True Vampire Story*, about the sensational crime.

THE BEGINNINGS OF A MOVEMENT

While stories of bloodthirsty teenage vampire clans roaming the countryside were few and far between in the 1990s, the "Vampire Cult Murders," as they came to be called, did succeed in drawing attention to an underground movement taking shape in America and Europe of modern-day vampires. As with the vampire myth itself, the origins of the movement are shrouded in mystery, but some twentieth-century authors gave reports of its presence in London in the 1930s.

Elliott O'Donnell, an Irish writer, ghost hunter, and spiritualist, mentions one such group in his 1935 book *Strange Cults and Secret Societies of Modern London*, in which he describes witnessing a vampire gathering in the basement of an old building, the floors and walls of which the cult had painted blood red. During the ceremony, a group of women dressed in long red gowns with red fingernails filed in. After eating an unknown flower, which O'Donnell's host claimed was from the Balkans, the women fell into a deep trance. Hours later when they reemerged from their meditative states, each claimed that they had entered the bedrooms of the cult's enemies in their astral forms and drained their victims of blood.

Unfortunately, there is little proof that such nefarious groups existed at the time, and O'Donnell was a rather colorful character with a reputation for never letting a few pesky facts get in the way of a good story. But if nothing else, then such tales do show us that the idea of, or at least fear of, such groups prevailed. This was, after all, a few short years after the premiere of Tod Browning's 1931 movie *Dracula*. Blend that with a twist of new-age spiritualism, and it's no wonder Londoners were seeing vampires lurking in every dark alley.

The first legitimate stirrings of a vampire movement seemed not to have begun until the 1970s as an offshoot of the rising interest in neo-Paganism and the desire by many disillusioned with traditional religious structures to explore alternative forms of spiritualism. Though none of these groups saw themselves as vampires and would have abhorred the negative label, some did incorporate the use of human blood in their magical rituals and ceremonies, giving power and precedence to its consumption. For instance, one magical grimoire or book of spells claims that writing the name of an enemy in animal's blood on a piece of parchment and then burning it with a black candle will bring about the death, illness, or sorrow of the spell's target.

Interestingly enough, some love spells also depend on the use of blood to perform, and require the magician to prick the middle finger of his or her right hand and use it to write the name of the intended lovers on a plain white piece of paper in the form of a circle. Three additional circles are then formed around the names, and the paper is buried outside at exactly nine o'clock at night (González-Wippler, 164).

In addition to this popularization of alternative spiritual structures was a new and exciting wave of vampire fiction hitting the shelves, such as the works of Anne Rice, who cast her vampire protagonists in a more seductive and compelling light, making them more human than before. Latching on to the craze was a revival in vampire movies during the 1980s and 1990s that helped fuel the romantic appeal of the vampire myth. Now, vampire enthusiasts didn't just want to be scared by vampires—they wanted to be vampires. No longer as isolated by their interests, vampire enthusiasts began to form loose networks or groups around self-published news-letters and magazines devoted to vampirism and blood play, with names such as *Necropolis*, *VAMPS*, and *Crimson*.

Nightclubs started featuring vampire nights, and a new wave of vampire-styled musical groups burst onto the scene, creating a unique underground movement unlike anything seen before. Some groups were directly inspired by the works of Anne Rice, including the gothic industrial band Lestat, whose first release, *Theatre of the Vampires*, debuted in 1990. Many other groups caught the dark wave also and either featured band members who openly claimed to be vampires, like Vlad's Dark Theater, or whose lyrics resonated vampire-styled themes, such as Bauhaus, the Sisters of Mercy, Rob Zombie, and Type O Negative. Even some mainstream artists belted out vampire-inspired tunes, as with Sting's song "Moon over Bourbon Street," about a vampire cruising the streets of New Orleans.

By the time the Internet rolled around, the community was ready to explode. Enthusiasm in vampirism soared to new heights as the age of information ushered in thousands of chat rooms and websites where vampires and those interested in them could meet, mingle, and exchange ideas. It also meant that to some degree the movement lost its underground edge to the voracious beast of consumerism. Amusingly, one indicator of its new status was the rise in vampire-themed weddings in Las Vegas. For the price of a few poker chips, a half-inebriated couple could stumble in off the Strip and be married by a guy with plastic fangs and a cheap vampire suit, all to the scratchy sounds of recorded organ music piped out of a loudspeaker.

VAMPYRES

When understanding the modern vampire movement, it is important to make the distinction that it draws very little from the creature's folkloric past, but rather relies on a reinvention of the myth to suit its own purposes—a thought that would make any eighteenth-century Eastern European peasant drop his pitchfork and torch in disbelief. Yet who could blame modern vampire enthusiasts? After all, no one wants to emulate a bloated, disease-ridden corpse stumbling about in the night covered in grave dirt and blood like some mindless zombie. In fact, when referring to themselves, many modern vampires prefer to spell the word *vampire* with a *y*, as *vampyre*, in order to separate themselves from the revenants of Eastern European tradition.

Outside of the obvious pop culture influences of film, television, and novels, two unique trends developed to help shape the image of the vampire in the twentieth century. The first can be found in the occult writings of earlier, nineteenth-century spiritualists who broadened the concept of the vampire from a primitive blood drinker to a being with an astral nature that fed off the energy of others. This in turn opened the door for those who wished to pursue a vampiric lifestyle but were far too squeamish to engage in the traditional blood play that qualified them as one of the new living undead. The second trend was the introduction of live action roleplaying games, or LARPs, onto the scene. As an offshoot of the popular Dungeons & Dragons roleplaying game, first published in 1974, LARPs took roleplaying to a new level, placing the gamer physically in the role of their character and requiring that they act out their responses in order to win the game.

In 1991 the LARP *Vampire: The Masquerade* by White Wolf Games was published, taking as its theme a world in which postmodern vampires interact with one another through various clans to which they owe allegiance. The result was two-fold. First, it provided a venue by which those interested in a vampyre lifestyle could interact and play out their fantasies. The second result was altogether unexpected, in that the fantasy game began to inspire new traditions or ideals in the vampire mythology unlike anything seen before, proving that in some cases life does imitate art.

For instance, the game is based on a series of rules that govern the interaction of the players; taking their lead from the game, many modern vampires adopted an ethical system known as the *Black Veil 2.0* or "The 13 Rules of the Community." As published in Michelle Belanger's book *The Psychic Vampire Codex*, these guidelines spell out how vampyres are to treat each other and members of mainstream society. Several of these rules emphasize that discretion should be exercised at all times—both when revealing one's self to the outside world and during blood play. Other rules state that donors should be treated with respect and never harmed either physically or emotionally, and that the utmost safety precautions should be used when drinking another's blood. Finally, each vampire community has its own rules and hierarchy, which must be respected by members of other communities (Belanger 2004, 265–68).

While some within the subculture have criticized the list as being too closely associated with the roleplaying game that spawned it, others claim it provides a systematic overview within the community, stressing qualities such as respect, safety, diversity, and responsibility.

Lifestyle Vampyres

Although the term *vampyre* in its modern sense is a catch-all phrase for a wide range of practices and beliefs, there are two important types that deserve further examination. The first is perhaps the most numerous, and participants in this group are known as *lifestyle vampyres*, because while they do not believe they are actual vampires, they are fascinated with everything associated with the topic. Many dress in dark or Victorian-style clothing, lighten their skin with makeup, or wear special contact lenses and prosthetic fangs. Some diehards even go as far as to sleep in a coffin at night to get the full effect.

While the majority do not consume human blood, some engage in the practice on occasion out of curiosity, as part of a group ritual, or as a form of eroticism. Lifestyle and other vampyres often claim that they live in two worlds or have two natures, consisting of a dayside and a nightside persona. During the day many hold regular jobs as teachers, construction workers, or doctors. At night, however, they don their vampire clothing, pop in their fangs, and mingle with others of their kind at vampyre clubs or other similarly themed establishments.

Real Vampyres

The second type of vampyre includes those who do not define themselves by their style of dress or may not even associate with other vampyres, but who believe that they must feed off the blood or energy of others in order to survive. Members of this group, whom we'll call *real vampyres*, see their vampirism as something inherent to their genetic makeup rather than a choice they make. While some resent their cravings and the social stigma it places on them, others have come to accept the need as a normal part of their lives. A few even believe that the act of feeding from another human gives them supernatural powers, including heightened awareness, night vision, premonitions, mind reading, and aura perception.

This consuming need to feed often takes one of two forms: drinking the blood of a willing donor or absorbing some of their very life energy. Those who ingest human blood are often referred to as Sanguinarians and usually do so in very small amounts, because large quantities act as a natural emetic causing nausea and vomiting. They may feed anywhere from once every few months to daily depending on their need, but many real vampyres report that if they abstain for too long they grow physically weak or sick and in some rare cases can die.

Contrary to most movie images, real vampyres do not creep into open windows at night and bite beautiful young women on the neck. In fact, the human bite is one of the most unsanitary methods available and can lead to serious infection. Instead, real vampyres feed on willing donors by making a small incision in the skin with a medical lancet or razor just superficial enough to draw a small amount of blood but not deep enough to scar. There are of course risks involved in the practice, including the transmission of blood-borne pathogens such as hepatitis and HIV. Small groups of trusted vampyres and donors frequently form what are called *feeding circles* to help minimize the spread of such diseases. A portion even choose to feed on the blood of butchered meat when they cannot find a trusted donor or because they disdain human blood altogether, but this too carries its own set of problems. What's important to understand about real vampyres is their belief that blood carries within it a rejuvenating power, and while most find human blood a satisfying source, many believe the blood of another vampyre is more powerful because it carries within it the essences of those whose blood they consumed as well.

Another means of feeding is known as *psychic vampirism* and occurs when the vampyre feeds off the living essence, life force, or energy of another person. Many religious traditions, especially those with Eastern influences, believe that humans, and all living organisms for that matter, are in part comprised of invisible auric and pranic energy that acts as a vital living force running through the world. While psychic

vampyres only ethically feed in this manner from willing donors, much as their blood-drinking cousins, some less scru-
pulous choose to conduct their feedings on people who are
unaware that they are the target of a psychic attack.

The notion of psychic vampirism was first developed in
the spiritual circles of the nineteenth century by writers such
as Violet Mary Firth Evans, who used the pseudonym Dion
Fortune from her family's Latin motto *Deo, non fortuna* ("By
God, not fate"). In her 1930 work *Psychic Self-Defense*, she laid
the groundwork for this form of vampirism, claiming "that
psychic attacks are far commoner than generally realized,
even by occultists themselves"(p. xiv). Dion Fortune high-
lighted many cases of psychic vampire attacks and claimed to
have been the victim of several herself. More importantly for
the vampyre community that followed, she and other writers
like her removed the notion that vampires now and in the
past subsisted only on human blood.

Psychic vampirism is believed to occur on a number of levels, ranging from non-intrusive surface feedings where the
vampyre draws upon the faint cast-off energy of those around
them, to deep feedings in which they siphon large amounts of
energy from a single person. A few even claim the ability to
leave their body in astral form while asleep and seek out victims whom they feed upon remotely in dreams. Finally, some
are said to be completely unaware that they even possess the
ability and drain those around them unconsciously.

In Konstantinos' *Vampires: The Occult Truth*, the author and
occult expert recounts his own brush with a psychic vampyre
while at a party. After entering a mildly altered state of consciousness from exhaustion, Konstantinos gazed across the

room to an older woman sitting by herself and was horrified to find he could see her dark vampiric emanations, which he described as a "dark purple aura that emanated about two feet from her body. Towards its edges the aura seemed to darken so that it looked almost black, yet the darkened area did not prevent me from seeing through it to the purple area. From the dark edge of the aura, several thin, black tentacles were protruding and moving towards the group of party guests" (Konstantinos 1996, 148).

Some conditions require that all a vampyre has to do is sit in a crowded room and soak up the ambient energy around them, while at other times the vampyre can imagine a tendril of psychic energy extending from their body towards another person, which latches on to their victim's being and drains it of energy. Usually after a vampyre is done feeding, the donor or victim may experience fatigue or exhaustion and on some occasions even illness or worse, while juxtaposed to this the vampyre is left refreshed and rejuvenated. We've all known people who leave us mentally and emotionally drained after spending any length of time with them just as they seem to become more energized by our presence, never realizing that we may have been the victim of a psychic assault.

As strange as many of these practices may seem to some, it's important to note that although lifestyle vampyres and real vampyres represent the vast majority of the vampyre subculture, there are other variations or hybrid groups mixing at various levels with everything from gothic to punk to sadomasochistic eroticism. Even within the major groups that represent the modern vampyre there is much overlap, and distinguishing between a real fang and a fake fang can be difficult at times. While interest in vampires will always cycle between periods of dormancy and sheer mania, it's exciting to watch the new face of the vampire being applied by modern enthusiasts, adding yet another chapter to the creature's legend.

Hence as long as one believes that the evil man wears horns, one will not discover an evil man.

—ERICH FROMM, *THE ANATOMY OF HUMAN DESTRUCTIVENESS*

8

THE BLOOD DRINKER NEXT DOOR

Sitting like a pale specter in the dark sky, the gibbous moon wanes high overhead as you make your way through the twisting streets of the neighborhood. In another twenty minutes you'll be back at home sitting in front of the television watching your favorite sitcom and thinking about work tomorrow. For now the crisp air muffles the sounds of your cadence, and the occasional noise of a distant dog barking is the only thing that seems to break the silence. Rounding Elm Street you quicken the pace, knowing that you're about to enter a section that most other residents shy away from even during the daylight. Weed-choked lots spring up where houses once stood, and the few that do remain sit like quiet sleepers with their shades tightly drawn.

A twisted wrought-iron fence begins on your left, and although you would rather not look, you still glimpse the forms of the fading tombstones and moldering crypts beyond that make up Oakwood Cemetery. Of course as an adult you don't believe in ghosts or other such nonsense, but the place does have its share of creepy tales, and walking past it at night alone does nothing to keep the hairs on the back of your neck from standing up. Moving your legs faster, you break into a nervous run past the massive gates that mark its entrance until you round another corner, losing it from sight. With aching lungs and burning muscles you eventually slow to a walk again, giving yourself time to get your heart back under control. Now that the fear is gone, you cannot help but smile at the thought of how childish it all seems. You blame your grandmother for filling your head with all those stories about vampires lurking around cemeteries just waiting to pounce on naughty little children.

Lost in your thoughts, you hardly notice the car coming up from behind until it pulls to a stop next to you. Its murky interior seems impenetrable in the darkness, and just as your brain begins to flash its warning signals the window rolls down and out pops the smiling face of your next-door neighbor, Mr. Johnson.

"Out for an evening stroll, I see," he beams at you.

"Ye … yes," you stutter in obvious relief. "But I'm a little winded right now."

"Well, by all means, then, hop in, and I'll give you a ride home," he offers.

You hesitate at first, looking back to the bend that leads past the cemetery once more. After all, he is your next-door neighbor, right? You've seen him going to church on Sundays;

he always keeps his yard nice; and he has a wife and kids. Bending low to enter the dark car, you think how lucky you are not to have to run past that creepy cemetery again, never realizing that the real monster is sitting in the seat next to you, smiling and adjusting the mirror as he pulls away from the curb and drives off into the night.

Days later the authorities will find your lifeless body, drained of all its blood, in a ditch not far from the cemetery, and although they have no suspects the local paper will run sinister headlines such as "Vampire Killer on the Loose," or "Body Found Drained of Blood." Not long afterwards, Mr. Johnson will be out in his yard pruning his rose bushes, and a neighbor will stroll by and make small talk before commenting on what a tragedy it is that someone from the block was murdered. Then Mr. Johnson will pause, smile his toothy grin, and say, "Why, yes, whoever did such a thing must be a real monster indeed."

Throughout our ghoulish examination of the vampire, we've traveled to many exotic lands and delved deep into the past to hunt down some of the world's most notorious blood drinkers. During this journey we've encountered some of the creature's most frightening incarnations, but as impossible as it seems, we have yet to examine one of its most insidious—and therefore most dangerous—forms.

The worst of these infernal monsters do not have fangs, rest in graves during the day, or run screaming from crucifixes; nor do they have Hollywood movies made about them. Instead, they hold normal jobs, live in quiet neighborhoods, pay their taxes, and drive fuel-efficient cars. They live not on the fringe of society creeping around graveyards at night, but rather they hide in broad daylight, making themselves indistinguishable from the rest of us. The most diabolical vampires are not those whispered about in the superstitions of Eastern European peasantry, but rather the ones who live right next door to you.

FRI+Z HAARꟼANN

Take, for example, the infamous Fritz Heinrich Karl Haarmann, whom the German press came in the 1920s to dub the "Vampire of Hannover." Born in the city of Hannover in Lower Saxony on October 25, 1879, Haarmann was the unassuming sixth child of a stern and impoverished German family. In fact, there is little to say at all about his early life until 1898, when he came to the attention of authorities after he was arrested on the charge of child molestation. In lieu of prison, however, doctors found him mentally unfit to stand trial and transferred him to a psychiatric intuition, where he stayed a few brief months before escaping and fleeing across the border into Switzerland.

After several years on the run, Haarmann returned to Germany and enlisted in the army under an alias; yet despite being listed as a good soldier, he was discharged in 1903 with neurasthenia, an early medical term for mental exhaustion. Haarmann returned to Hannover, where the authorities incredulously seemed to have forgotten all about his past, and for the next decade he found himself in and out of jail for petty crimes ranging from theft to fraud. During this period his run-ins with the police allowed him the advantage of becoming a low-level informant, which he later used to deflect their attention away from his own activities. In addition to his criminal activities, he also learned a trade as a butcher and opened a shop in the seamy underbelly of the city's Old Quarter, where few questions were ever asked and even fewer answers given.

It wasn't until September of 1918, however, during a time when Germany languished under a harsh economic depression just weeks before its conclusive defeat in World War I, that he committed the first of a long string of murders by taking the life of a seventeen-year-old boy named Friedel Rothe. At the time police knew only that the boy had gone missing and was last seen in Haarmann's company, but when Friedel's family began clamoring for answers, officials raided Haarmann's apartment, where they found Haarmann with a semi-naked, underage boy. Although no evidence surfaced as to Friedel's whereabouts, Haarmann was charged with the sexual assault of the young boy found in his apartment and sentenced to nine months in prison.

A year later and back on the streets of Hannover, Haarmann met a young runaway named Hans Grans, who was working as a male prostitute. The two became lovers and moved into Haarmann's old apartment together, where Haarmann hatched the deadly scheme of luring runaways back to their quarters to be stripped of their belongings and murdered. He put the plan into action by prowling the railway stations at night looking for destitute boys sleeping on the platforms. After finding one he was attracted to, he would awaken him with a forceful nudge of his boot, and under the guise of being a station manager or rail detective demand to see his ticket.

If the boy was unable to produce a ticket (which was usually the case), Haarmann feigned sympathy for his plight and invited the boy back to his apartment, where Haarmann filled him with food, wine, and the promise of a warm bed. Once the boy's head was swimming with too much alcohol, Haarmann sprang his trap, and with a sudden leap he would grab the boy from behind, tearing open the boy's throat with his teeth, then raping him and drinking his blood.

Haarmann would later clean up the evidence, pawn the victim's belongings, and butcher the body to be sold as salted pork on the black market, in what can only be compared in gruesomeness to something from *Sweeney Todd: The Demon Barber of Fleet Street*. What portions proved not to be disposable Haarmann weighed down with rocks and dumped into the nearby Leine River, which in June of 1924 led to his undoing after a bag of human remains washed ashore. After dragging the river for days, the police discovered nearly five hundred human bones belonging to what they believed were twenty-two separate victims.

Given Haarmann's history as a sexual predator in the community and his questionable involvement in the disappearance of Friedel Rothe, he became number one on their list of suspects and was placed under constant surveillance. Authorities would not have to wait long, though. True to his nature, he was soon arrested for trying to lure yet another teenaged boy back to his apartment. In a search of his residence, police were horrified to find its walls splattered with blood and items belonging to his victims neatly kept as souvenirs.

Under interrogation, Haarmann estimated he had murdered as many as fifty to seventy young boys (he would be convicted of murdering twenty-four), referring to them in his shocking confession as "game," and went on to implicate his accomplice Hans Grans in the crimes as well. The trial that followed became a sensation across Germany, and on December 19, 1924, Fritz Haarmann was convicted of twenty-four separate counts of murder and sentenced to death. While he oddly pleaded to be decapitated with a long sword in the town market, his life was instead ended four months later under a guillotine's blade behind the walls of Hannover prison. His brain was removed and shipped to the Göttingen Medical Hospital for study, where it rests to this day in a jar of formaldehyde. Initially Hans Grans was also sentenced to death, but after a second trial his penalty was reduced to twelve years, and he died in Hannover in 1975.

BÉLA KISS

While Fritz Haarmann was still alive and stalking the cobblestone streets of Hannover, another monster was plying his bloody trade in a land not far to the east. For all intents and purposes, Béla Kiss appeared on the surface to be nothing more than a simple tinsmith. Although few facts are known about his early life, we do know that he was born in 1877, and in 1900 he moved into a rented cottage in Cinkota, just outside of Budapest, Hungary, where he set up shop as a tradesman.

Well liked by everyone in the town, Béla Kiss was a self-taught man who spent large amounts of time reading anything he could get his hands on. He also had quite the reputation as a ladies' man, and a number of attractive women were seen in his company from time to time. While the envy of most men, married or not, it was equally noticeable that his female companions didn't seem to last long, and before anyone knew it, they were gone.

In 1914 war broke out, and at the age of thirty-seven Béla Kiss joined the Hungarian army and marched off to the battlefields of Europe along with most of the other men from the town. As the news from the front remained grim, many in town guessed that he, like countless others, must have ended up either dead in a muddy trench somewhere or a prisoner of war. His landlord, reasoning he would surely never return, remembered that Béla Kiss had kept a number of large drums behind his house that he claimed were for storing petrol.

Hoping to profit from the abandoned cache, the landlord punctured one of the drums, but instead of the smell of gasoline he was greeted with the overpowering odor of rotting flesh. Fearing the worst he called in the local police, who led by Detective Chief Charles Nagy removed the drum's lid and found the naked body of a young woman preserved in wood alcohol. Six more drums were opened, and in each the same gruesome sight awaited. Later autopsies revealed that each of the women had been strangled to death with a rope, but lending an even more macabre element to the case was that they all had two small puncture marks on their necks and were completely drained of blood.

With this discovery Detective Nagy and his men combed the rest of the house and property, finding an additional seventeen bodies, all of which bore the same causes of death and evidence of exsanguination. Some were buried about the yard while others were simply stacked like cord wood in a nearby tool shed. In one part of the house, officials even found a secret room containing countless letters between Béla Kiss and numerous women. By the looks of it, Detective Nagy surmised, the silver-tongued Kiss had been enticing women to his home for years with promises of marriage and then murdering them.

Catching such a clever killer proved harder than police could ever have imagined, however, since Béla Kiss was presumed killed or captured on the front. Nagy alerted the military nonetheless and ordered the arrest of Kiss, but on October 4, 1916, he received a letter from the commandant of a Serbian hospital with the news that his fugitive had died of typhoid. Initially it seemed that the "Monster of Cinkota" had escaped justice, but soon after the first letter a second correspondence arrived from the hospital stating that a mistake had been made and that he was alive after all and recuperating. With the news in hand, military officials rushed to the infirmary ward only to find that the body in his bed was not that of Béla Kiss, but rather a soldier who had died shortly before. It appeared that Kiss was tipped off somehow and substituted a dead body for his own before disappearing.

For years the Hungarian police continued to receive sightings of Béla Kiss from around Europe and even from as far away as America. Some claimed that he had been jailed in Romania for theft, others that he died of yellow fever in Turkey. In the 1920s he was said to be a soldier in the French Foreign Legion, and in 1932 he was even reportedly spotted in Times Square, New York, working as a janitor. In each of these cases the reports were either untrue or the suspect vanished prior to questioning, and the trail went cold. Who exactly Béla Kiss was, where he went, and why he drained his victims of their blood in such a peculiar manner are answers that are forever lost to us.

RICHARD CHASE

If one were to assume that such vile acts were only committed by people who lived long ago, one would be dangerously wrong. A more modern case is that of Richard Trenton Chase, the "Vampire of Sacramento," who in late 1977 and early 1978 murdered six innocent people and drank their blood. While Chase's life started off as normally as any other, he began showing signs of mental illness in early adolescence, including a bizarre hypochondria concerned with the functioning of his internal organs. By adulthood he was abusing drugs and alcohol frequently and had developed a curious obsession for consuming blood, based on the delusion that if he did not, his body would disintegrate.

In 1975 this psychosis led to his hospitalization with blood poisoning after injecting rabbit's blood into his veins. Following a psychiatric examination, Chase was admitted to a mental institution called the Beverly Manor. During his stay at the "Manor," he freely shared with doctors his morbid fantasies of killing animals and drinking their blood and earned the nickname Dracula after staff found dead birds in his room and fresh blood around his mouth. After a year of observation, counseling, and psychotropic medication, doctors were convinced he was no longer a threat and released him to his parents' conservatorship. Back on the streets, however, his overprotective mother had a different opinion on her son's course of treatment, and without his doctor's knowledge she moved him into an apartment of his own and began weaning him off his medication.

This of course proved disastrous, and before long Richard Chase was spiraling down into madness and bloodlust once again. On August 3, 1977, officers of the Bureau of

Indian Affairs at the Pyramid Lake Indian Reservation found Chase wandering nude and covered in blood. Not far away they discovered his Ford Ranchero stuck in the sand with several rifles, a pile of men's clothing, and a liver (which was determined to belong to a cow) in the front seat. Although Chase was not arrested or charged with any crime, the incident proved a sinister prelude of the violence yet to come.

Months later he took his first victim when he drove by the East Sacramento home of fifty-one-year-old Edward Griffin and shot him dead while he was unloading groceries from his car. Law enforcement's lack of headway in the murder only seemed to fuel Chase's psychosis, and over the next month he randomly killed five more people. When later asked by FBI agents how he chose his victims, Chase explained that he merely walked down the street testing whether or not people had locked their front doors. If they were locked, he recounted, he knew he was not welcome and so he moved on to the next house.

The last of his murders occurred on January 27, 1978, when he entered the home of thirty-eight-year-old Evelyn Miroth in the middle of the day. In the rampage that followed, Evelyn Miroth; her friend Danny Meredith; Evelyn's six-year-old son, Jason; and her twenty-two-month-old nephew were shot to death with a .22 caliber handgun. After mutilating the corpses and drinking their blood, Chase engaged in necrophilia with Evelyn's body. Startled by a knock at the door, Chase fled the scene, but not before leaving a trail of forensic evidence that quickly led to his arrest. While he was in custody, police searched his apartment, which they reported looked more like a slaughterhouse than a domicile; blood covered everything from the furniture in the living room to the food in the refrigerator. Even more ominous was the discovery of a calendar marking the dates of his murders, with forty-one more planned in the year to come.

On May 8, 1979, Richard Chase was found guilty of six counts of murder in the first degree and sentenced to die in the California gas chamber. But before his sentence could be carried out, he escaped justice by taking his own life. At the age of thirty, the "Vampire of Sacramento" was found dead in his cell in San Quentin from an overdose of antidepressants he had allegedly been saving for weeks.

JAMES RIVA

Despite the fact that the men mentioned so far in this chapter became known for their propensity to drink or drain their victims of blood, none of these killers actually considered themselves vampires in the literal sense. Yet there have been some blood drinkers who have cast themselves in the mantle of the vampire and committed unspeakable acts of savagery to pursue their need for blood.

On April 10, 1980, twenty-two-year-old James Riva of Marshfield, Massachusetts, shot and killed his handicapped grandmother with bullets he painted gold. After trying to drink the blood from her wounds, he dosed her body in antifreeze and gasoline and set it on fire. When he later confessed his crime to police, he defended his actions by claiming self-defense. His grandmother, he maintained, was a vampire who had been secretly poisoning his food and using an ice pick while he slept to drink his blood. According to Riva's delusion, everyone in the world was covertly a vampire but himself and if he killed and drank the blood of another, he, too, would become a vampire and all the other vampires would throw him a party.

Fascinated with vampires from the age of thirteen, Riva began displaying signs of mental illness from an early age and was known to obsess over drawing pictures depicting acts of violence and gore. In time this urge led to his killing and drinking the blood of small animals. During his pretrial psychiatric review, he also reported that he kept an axe near his bedroom door and that he planned to kill his father with it one day.

Although his defense attorneys brought in a host of psychiatric doctors who diagnosed him with paranoid schizophrenia, he was nonetheless found guilty of second-degree murder and arson and sentenced to life in prison. On August 4, 2009, James Riva went before the Massachusetts state parole board after twenty-nine years of incarceration and testified that he was rehabilitated and ready for release back into society. Prison officials were not as convinced, however, and stated that he could not be trusted off of his medication. During an incident they recounted, Riva attacked a prison guard who he believed was sneaking into his cell at night and stealing his spinal fluid. Subsequently, Riva was not granted parole.

ALLAN MENZIES

Although James Riva feared the thought of vampires, his crimes, according to his faulty reasoning, were actually intended to make him one of them, demonstrating that for some the lure of the vampire can be exceedingly strong, turning a mild interest into a deadly desire. Take, for example, the well-publicized case of twenty-two-year-old Allan Menzies of Fauldhouse, West Lothian, Scotland, who in December of 2002 killed his childhood friend of eighteen years and drank his blood, believing that doing so would make him an immortal vampire.

Prior to the killing, Menzies became engrossed in the vampire film *Queen of the Damned*, adapted from a novel by Anne Rice. In it, the scantily clad vampire queen Akasha rises from her ancient slumber to feed not only on the blood of the living but on the blood of her fellow vampires as well. Fixated on the film and its main character, Menzies spent long periods of time locked in his room watching the movie over and over again. His father later told police that he often heard his son talking to himself while alone in his room and that on more than one occasion he began shouting as if in a heated argument with someone. During the periods when Menzies did venture out of his room, which were becoming less frequent, he was consumed with talking about roleplaying games and vampires and often spoke as if the character Akasha were a real person.

Then, on December 11, 2002, twenty-one-year-old Thomas McKendrick disappeared after last being seen in the Menzies' home. That same day, Allan Menzies' father returned from work to find suspicious bloodstains throughout the house, which Allan explained occurred after he sliced his hand opening a can of dog food. Although Menzies' father seemed satisfied with this explanation, the Scottish police were not, but with no evidence of foul play there was little that could be done. That is, until a few weeks later when what started as a missing person's case suddenly escalated into murder after the decomposing body of McKendrick was discovered buried in a shallow grave in the forest not far from the Menzies home. The autopsy revealed that McKendrick had been brutally stabbed forty-two times in the face, neck, and shoulders, and had been beaten repeatedly with a hammer-like object.

The police were quick to respond and immediately took Allan Menzies into custody, where they questioned him about the death of his friend McKendrick. To their surprise Menzies made no pretense at duplicity and readily admitted to murdering his friend, calmly recounting the events as they unfolded on the day in question. According to Menzies' statement, the two men were talking in the kitchen of the Menzies home when McKendrick made a lewd comment about the actress who played Akasha in the film *Queen of the Damned*. Menzies, who was slicing a raw liver at the time, took a large bowie knife and attacked his friend, stabbing him and then beating him with a hammer until long after he stopped moving. When the act was finished, Menzies drank two cups' worth of blood from the wounds of his dead friend and ate a small piece of his brain. During the killing, he claimed, his beloved vampire queen looked on, encouraging his murderous actions.

In their search of the crime scene, police found a copy of the movie *Queen of the Damned* and a frayed vampire novel, *Blood and Gold* by Anne Rice. In the book were scribbled numerous handwritten notes by Menzies pointing to something far more than just a simple case of jealous murder, including one that read, "The master will come for me and he has promised to make me immortal … I have chosen my fate to become a vampire, blood is much too precious to be wasted on humans … the blood is the life, I have drank the blood, and it shall be mine for I have seen horror" (Robertson 2003).

In court Menzies pled guilty to culpable homicide on the grounds of diminished responsibility, but the crown rejected his plea and ordered him to stand trial before the high court in Edinburgh, where he was sentenced to life in prison with a minimum of eighteen years. In November of 2004 he was found dead in his cell at Shotts Prison of an apparent suicide.

DANIEL AND MANUELA RUDA

Noticeably, while most of those mentioned in this chapter acted alone (although Haarmann had an accomplice to hide the evidence, he nevertheless committed the murders by himself), there are rare occasions when blood drinkers commit their crimes in concert with one another. On January 31, 2002, a young husband and wife were convicted in a German court of law for the murder of a thirty-three-year-old man named Frank Hackert in the town of Witten. According to court records, the two lured the unsuspecting man to their apartment under the pretense of a party and stabbed him to death. When the deed was finished, they ritualistically carved a pentagram on his chest and drank his blood before falling asleep together in a coffin next to his body.

Daniel Ruda and his wife, Manuela, first met through the personals in a heavy metal magazine called *Metal-Hammer*, where he placed an ad reading, "Black-haired vampire seeks princess of darkness who despises everything and everybody and has bidden farewell to life" (Rowlatt 2002).

Although both were avowed Satanists, they were also participating members of the vampyre community. Manuela claimed that, at the age of fourteen, the devil first began speaking to her and reassuring her that he had chosen her for something special. A few years later she left her hometown of Witten and traveled to the Scottish Highlands, where she spent her time wandering lonely graveyards and absorbing the gloomy atmosphere. For a while she even lived in a cave on the isolated Isle of Skye. She also lived in London, where she worked in a popular gothic club. It was here that she joined her first vampyre coven and began attending "bite parties," developing a taste for human blood.

During the trial the defendants showed little regard for their victim's family and often acted out in front of the press with rude gestures and strange antics, turning the whole affair into a media circus. Manuela even insisted at one point that the judge blacken the windows of the courtroom to hide the sun; a request he denied, of course. Nonetheless, the publicity that followed the deadly couple turned them into overnight media personalities, and fan mail from deranged fans flooded into the jail where they were being kept.

Both Daniel and Manuela admitted to the murder but refused to plead guilty, on the grounds that they were only following the orders of their master Lucifer and were therefore not to blame. They went on to recount that after the murder they planned to commit suicide in a cemetery and send their souls to hell, where they would be granted an exalted place among the damned. Instead, they were captured by police outside a gas station, armed with a chainsaw that they planned to use to further their body count.

Psychiatric experts diagnosed the two with a severe narcissistic personality disorder, and predicted that if freed they would undoubtedly kill again. Despite this obvious assessment of their future intentions, the German court only gave Daniel and Manuela Ruda fifteen and thirteen years respectively, and committed them to a hospital for the criminally insane.

THE ⊕+HERS

Although the handful of cases examined thus far certainly represent a fair sampling of crimes committed by the most dangerous blood drinkers, they still only touch on a small portion of the bloody acts carried out through history. Other dark examples include:

- Martin Dumollard, a Frenchman who killed and drank the blood of several girls in the mid-nineteenth century.

- Eusebius Pieydagnelle, who killed six women in France in 1878, after the smell of blood from a nearby butcher's shop excited him.

- Joseph Vacher, who drank the blood of a dozen murder victims in southeastern France in the 1890s.

- The "Monster of Düsseldorf," Peter Kürten, who in the late 1920s committed thirteen murders. He drank the blood of many of his victims.

- Magdalena Solís, the "High Priestess of Blood," who in the early 1960s convinced villagers in Mexico that she was an Inca goddess and instigated numerous blood rituals involving the murders of eight people.

- The "Podlaski Vampire," Julian Koltun, who in the early 1980s raped, murdered, and drank the blood of a number of women.

- John Crutchley, the so-called "Vampire Rapist," who in Florida in 1985 held a teenaged girl prisoner in order to rape her and drain her of blood, which he drank.

- Andrei Chikatilo, a sadistic serial killer who murdered over fifty people in the former Soviet Union from 1978 to 1990. In some of these murders, he confessed to eating his victims' body parts and drinking their blood.

- Marcelo Costa de Andrade, the "Vampire of Niterói," who in the early 1990s killed fourteen young boys in Rio de Janeiro and drank their blood in order to become as "young and pretty" as they were.

- Deborah Jean Finch, a woman living in Santa Cruz, California, who murdered and drank the blood of a man named Brandon McMichaels in 1991.

- Joshua Rudiger, the "Vampire Slasher," who killed a homeless woman in San Francisco, and injured three homeless men, all by slashing their necks in order to imbibe their blood. Rudiger believed he was a 2,600-year-old vampire.

This list could go on until there is no more stomach for it, as more join the ranks of those before them. But as frightening as it truly is, the most dangerous men and women are those who have plied their bloody trade unnoticed and have therefore failed to make the list. Again and again, the thirst for blood has cut across time, culture, and even gender, suggesting that the preoccupation harkens back through history to humanity's earliest beginnings.

As we have seen, even in our enlightened age of sensibility and access to information, there are still some who hunt their fellow man like solitary beasts preying on the weak and unsuspecting. There are also some who have immersed themselves in the vampire mythology to the point of committing unspeakable acts against humanity in the belief that they too will share in the mystery and darkness that is the vampire. Although reasons and methods vary from killer to killer, the twisted aim is the same: to taste human blood and the age-old forbidden power that courses through it.

The blood is the life! The blood is the life!

—BRAM STOKER, *DRACULA*

9

SOMETHING
IN THE BLOOD

Throughout history, vampires have been portrayed as the destroyers of crops, the murderers of infants, the bringers of nightmares, and the carriers of plagues, but for all their evil machinations it is perhaps their desire for human blood that above all else causes people to fear their name. Regardless of whether they appear in the rural hamlets of Eastern Europe or the sweltering jungle temples of the Indian subcontinent, it is the power of blood that animates and drives them to claw their way out of festering graves and feast upon the living. In order to truly understand the vampire, therefore, or any blood drinker within the pantheon, it is important to examine humanity's own beliefs about blood and how its consumption came to be attributed to these creatures.

Modern medical books define blood as a specialized fluid filled with plasma, blood cells, and platelets circulated by the heart through the body's vascular system with the task of carrying oxygen and nutrients to the body's tissue while moving harmful waste away to be disposed. The average adult has as much as 1.3 gallons (five liters) of blood coursing through their system at any one time, which accounts for 8 percent of their body weight. Hemoglobin within the blood gives the fluid its distinctive bright red color when exposed to the air, but when present in the veins it appears as a dark bluish red.

Yet does a textbook explanation hold the key to the vampire's seeming fascination with blood, or does the answer lie somewhere beyond the current understanding of mere science?

EARLY BELIEFS

We can only imagine what prehistoric people, observing the natural world around them, first thought when faced with the mystery of blood and how they wrestled with its connection to life and death. Perhaps the process began after noticing how a wounded deer stopped struggling when it lost too much blood or how one of their own tribesmen closed his eyes and ceased moving after being wounded in a skirmish with rivals. Modern archeological evidence suggests that even the Neanderthals of Europe and Western Asia 130,000 years ago understood the importance of blood in the life/death cycle and attributed a mystical quality to it.

On September 17, 1909, under a rock shelter in the Dordogne Valley of France, archeologists unearthed the bodies of eight Neanderthal skeletons buried in what appeared to be a highly ritualized manner. All of the fossilized remains were covered in a red pigment, which experts surmise was a primitive funerary custom linking the ideas of blood, warmth, and life together for those traveling to the afterlife.

As the eons passed and the earth's ice ages came and went, a Neolithic revolution occurred that allowed people to develop agriculture and permanent settlements. Through this series of events, people also found the need to account for the foundation of the world they lived in and the origins of the gods they worshiped. As part of these creation myths, there often existed the theme that blood provided the original spark by which life was created. For instance, in 1849 the British archeologist Austen Henry Layard discovered seven clay tablets from the royal library of Ashurbanipal, in the ruins of Nineveh, which contained the story of *Enuma Elish*, or, to Western scholars, *the Chaldean Genesis*.

This ancient Akkadian tale, which was old even at the time of its writing in the seventh century BCE, is a recounting of the struggle between the cosmic forces of order led by the chief god Marduk and those of chaos under the command of the evil sea goddess Tiamat, who appears as a fierce dragon. The two sides clash in a contest that shakes the very heavens, until Marduk at last triumphs over Tiamat, taking her body and ripping it in two in order to form the earth and sky. As punishment for ending up on the losing side of a divine war, Marduk has Tiamat's husband, Kingu, seized and his veins sliced open, letting the blood spill upon the newly created earth to become the first humans. The culmination of the tale, as translated by George Smith in 1876, was dramatically captured in the lines:

> They bound him, holding him before Ea.
> They imposed on him his guilt, and severed his blood (vessels).
> Out of his blood they fashioned mankind. (Reid 1987, 9)

A similar myth was told by the Nez Perce, a tribe of Native Americans who once inhabited what is today the Pacific Northwest of the United States. In their creation myth a gigantic monster came down from the north one day and began devouring all the plants and animals in the land. Fearing it would consume the entire world if not stopped, the great coyote bravely jumped into the monster's mouth and raced down into its belly. Once there he built a fire and cut out the heart of the beast with a flint knife, ending its life. Emerging from the body, the coyote began cutting it into pieces, each of which became a different tribe of men. When he was finished he washed the blood from his hands, which transformed upon hitting the water into the people of the Nez Perce (Leeming, 2010, 206–7).

F⊕⊕D F⊕R +HE G⊕DS

Blood and the shedding of it was a sacred act infused with the power to not only maintain life but to create it as well; for some cultures this also meant that it was a ready substance to be harnessed for their own ends when their priests needed to reach beyond the physical world and tap the power reservoirs of the spiritual. Many such groups came to practice ritual blood sacrifices for a variety of reasons. Among the Greeks, for instance, it was thought that the shades of the underworld relished the taste of blood and that through its consumption they grew strong enough to communicate with the living. In Homer's eighth-century BCE epic poem *The Odyssey*, the Greek hero of the tale, Odysseus, pays a visit to the witch of Crete to aid him in his quest to return home. She, however, advises him to seek the council of the shade Tiresias, who during his mortal life was a renowned soothsayer.

Odysseus travels to the very entrance of Hades but finds the spirits too weak to speak with him until he pours the blood of two butchered sheep into a shallow trench for them to feed upon. The result is immediate and described by Homer in chilling detail: "The ghosts came trooping up from Erebus—brides, young bachelors, old men worn out with toil, maids who had been crossed in love, and brave men who had been killed in battle, with their armor still smirched in blood; they came from every quarter and flitted round the trench with a strange kind of screaming sound that made me turn pale with fear" (Homer 1900, 140).

Other groups such as the Germanic Anglo-Saxons or the seafaring Norsemen also placed importance in the ritual spilling of blood during ceremonies known as *blot*, which in its verb form *blota* means "to worship with sacrifice." On these occasions animals such as cattle, pigs, or horses were sacrificed and boiled in large caldrons with heated stone. The meat was then shared among the participants, as well as the gods and spirits they believed were in attendance. The blood that had been collected was sprinkled on the statues of the local gods, the walls of buildings, weapons, and even the worshipers themselves. The act of sprinkling blood on objects for protection was called *bleodsian* in Old English, which in turn became the word *blessing* when the Roman Catholic Church adopted a watered-down version of the pagan rite.

Many other societies engaged in blood sacrifice, but some, like the ancient Druids of Gaul, practiced a form that only the power of human blood could provide. Very little is known of the enigmatic early Druids, since the only accounts of their activities are handed down from Greek and Roman writers who were themselves not averse to coloring their descriptions with conjecture and hearsay. What is known is that they were a priestly caste that came to power in Central and Western Europe during the Iron Age and that they engaged in an esoteric form of nature worship, which they passed down orally.

In the first century CE, the Roman poet Marcus Annaeus Lucanus wrote that Druids of Gaul (living near what is now Marseilles, France) sacrificed criminals, and other types of people when criminals were in short supply, in magical oak groves known as *nemetons* after the goddess Nemetona. These important religious sites were often enclosed in a wooden palisade or ditch and appeared throughout Gaul until the Roman invasions of the first century BCE. Those unfortunate enough to fall under the priest's knife had their blood ritually drained and sprinkled on the sacred oaks to imbue the trees with magical power. So feared were these places that it was said no birds nested in the trees nor wind stirred their leaves, and not even the heartiest priest would venture through the grove at midday or midnight lest he encounter one of its blood-drenched guardian spirits.

While many cultures engaged in human sacrifice during some portion of their history, none were as accomplished or as feared as the Aztec Empire, which dominated portions of Mesoamerica in the fourteenth, fifteenth, and early sixteenth centuries. Enemies captured in battle or given over as tribute from weaker vassal states made up the vast majority of the victims who met their end atop the Aztecs' blood-covered temples. While several gods within their pantheon demanded human blood, none was as voracious in their appetites as the sun god Huitzilopochtli, whose victims had their hearts torn from their chests with obsidian-bladed knifes and held aloft to the sky still beating. During the Aztec's reign of terror, it is estimated that as many as 20,000 prisoners a year were sacrificed (Hanson 2001, 195).

Critical to understanding the Aztec need for human blood was the concept of *tonalli*, or the animating spirit of a person, which was often linked to an animal spirit. This powerful interconnected totem became concentrated in the heart when the victim was frightened. Once released through sacrifice it was used by the sun god to continue his motion around the earth. Failing to appease the bloodthirsty god meant the sun would stop and the earth would end. To the warlike Aztecs, blood made the world go round, literally.

HEALING POWERS

Because of the mystical associations that blood had in many cultures, it was only natural that practitioners of the magical arts and early men of healing explored its curative powers. In the first century BCE, the Roman author and naturalist Pliny the Elder wrote that the pharaohs of Egypt bathed in the blood of humans to prevent leprosy. While such claims are questionable and suggest Roman disdain for cultures they felt were inferior to their own, this particular remedy against the disease later reappeared in a tale about the first Christian Emperor, Constantine the Great. In 337 CE after the feast of Easter, the great emperor fell seriously ill from an unknown disease and called upon his pagan Greek advisors for a remedy. Their prescription was that he bathe in the blood of murdered infants to exact a cure, a course of treatment he mercifully did not follow.

In the lands of the ancient Israelites, the remedy for leprosy included taking two live birds to the leper's home after a prescribed period of purification. The first bird was ritualistically killed and the second dipped into its blood. The remaining live bird was then used to sprinkle the leper seven times with the sacrificial blood before being let go to fly away. After a second period of purification, an unblemished male lamb was slaughtered and the blood wiped on the patient followed by a second sprinkling, this time with oil and wine.

Often the lengthy process was repeated many times before it was thought to produce results. Other blood cures involved the actual consumption of human blood to be effective, as in the case of the ancient Koreans who believed that the blood of a family's eldest son held magical healing powers. If a member of the household lay dying, the son in question opened his thigh with a blade and let the blood stream into a wooden bowl, which could then be used by local sorcerers to create healing elixirs guaranteed to restore the patient's health. Thousands of miles to the south, the Aboriginal people who lived near the Darling River in southeastern Australia practiced a similar custom, using the blood taken from the forearm of a friend instead.

Drawing blood or bloodletting was also used by early medical practitioners to treat a number of ailments, ranging from the common cold to more life-threatening diseases such as smallpox or tuberculosis. Blood was thought to be one of four "humors," along with black bile, yellow bile, and phlegm, that circulated through the body and were responsible for maintaining good health. When any one of these humors was out of balance they could lead to illness, disease, and even death. The cure then was to drain the excess fluid and return the body to its normal level. The custom of bloodletting is one of the oldest medical arts known to man and was implemented by numerous cultures throughout the world, including the early Mesopotamians, Egyptians, Greeks, Mayans, and Aztecs.

One of the most common methods was to puncture a large vein in the forearm or neck with a lancet and place a heated glass cup over the wound to create a vacuum and assist in draining the blood. At times leeches were used to the same effect, although they took longer to accomplish their goal. One rather wicked-looking device developed in the nineteenth century was known as a scarificator and consisted of a series of small blades spring-driven to cause many shallow cuts in the belief that it was more merciful than earlier methods. Normally between sixteen to thirty ounces of blood was collected at a time, and the procedure was repeated until the patient became faint.

Interestingly enough, in Europe during the Middle Ages both surgeons and barbers specialized in the custom. Barbers even advertised their services by hanging a red and white striped pole outside their place of business much as they do today. The pole itself represented the stick the patient squeezed to increase the blood flow, while the red stripe was for the blood being drained and the white stripe for the tourniquet the barber used to stop the bleeding.

Here in the United States, bloodletting arrived with English settlers on the Mayflower and continued to flourish until it lost favor in the nineteenth century. In 1799, before dying from a throat infection, it's known that George Washington was drained of nine pints of blood in a twenty-four-hour period, lending credence to the old saying that "sometimes the cure is worse than the disease."

THICKER THAN WATER

Since blood carried with it the profound connotations of the sacred and magical in humanity, it therefore became the link by which individuals and tribes bound themselves to one another. Before the invention of lawyers and contracts, the strongest oath a person could take was a blood oath, in which two parties mingled their blood together forming a mystical bond that could not be broken. To betray such a bond was a grievous sin and could only be equated with betraying one's own family, which in similar fashion was also bound by a biological blood tie.

Perhaps one of the most celebrated blood bonds known to history was recorded in the thirteenth-century Norwegian saga of Orvar-Oddr. In the tale, Orvar-Oddr decides to test his fighting skills against the renowned Swedish warrior Hjalmar and sets sail for the coast of Sweden with five ships of his best fighting men. Hjalmar, upon hearing of the approaching challenger, meets him on the high seas with fifteen of his own ships, but before the battle commences he sends ten of his ships home to even the odds. For two days the mighty forces clash until the sea ran red with the blood of dying men. Eventually the two great warriors fought to a draw, and realizing they were equals ceased their fighting to swear a blood oath to one another. Beaching their ships, the two men cut themselves and let their blood flow together while reciting oaths and incantations under a piece of turf held aloft by a spear. The two champions went on to fight many battles together until Hjalmar was finally killed in combat by the berserker Arngrim and his twelve sons.

The custom between warriors to form blood bonds was not limited to the northern European peoples but was a common element in many armies the world over—including ancient Greece, where whole companies of soldiers took such oaths to forge stronger fighting units. The practice was also found throughout those living in the Balkan Peninsula during the Ottoman era, where oppressed Christian populations struggled to maintain their sense of identity.

Among the fierce horsemen of Scythia, the custom was expressed by cutting themselves and allowing their blood to flow into a cup, which when mixed with wine they drank to seal the bond. In the Asiatic cultures farther east, the act of becoming someone's blood brother extended beyond the individual participants to include whole tribes and was seen as an effective means of bringing them into alliance with one another or to help resolve disputes. Even in today's world, where things hardly ever seem simple, the action of two people cutting their thumbs and pressing them together can still hold much significance.

BL⊕⊕D TAB⊕⊕S

While many early cultures developed ritualized practices associated with the handling of blood, some revered its power so much that they created strict laws and prohibitions against its usage. The Israelites, for example, believed that blood contained within it the very essence or life force of a creature—its soul if you will. Though animals could be sacrificed upon the temple's altar for the benefit of God, to actually consume blood, any blood, was a forbidden act. In the Book of Genesis 9:4, it is written that God spoke to Noah after the cataclysmic waters of the great flood had receded from the land and commanded that while he may eat the flesh of the animals, he "shall not eat flesh with its life, that is, with its blood." This admonition continued on into Mosaic Law, which later came to govern the Hebrew tribes, making the offense punishable by death. In turn this led to kosher dietary practices designed to avoid the consumption of blood, and even early Jewish hunters were commanded to pour out the blood of their kills onto the ground and cover it with dirt before they prepared their meat.

Of even greater consequence, however, was the wanton shedding of human blood, which unless sanctioned by God, was a horrid offense to the psyche of the Hebrews. In the story of Cain and Abel, when Cain slew his brother out of jealousy it was Abel's blood that cried out from the ground to accuse him of his sin before God. In the Hebrew Book of Numbers 35:33, this warning is sternly reinforced in the passage "You shall not pollute the land wherein you are, for blood it defiles the land, and the land cannot be cleansed of the blood that is shed therein, except by the blood of him that shed it."

In similar fashion many cultures felt it was particularly taboo to shed the blood of a member of a royal line or caste, and so they went to great lengths when disposing of their royalty to ensure that this did not happen. When the Great Mongolian conqueror Kublai Khan defeated his uncle Nayan in battle in 1287 CE, it is said that he executed his familial rival by wrapping him in a carpet and beating him to death lest the blood of his imperial line should spill upon the ground. This later gave rise to the old Tartar maxim: "One Khan will put another to death to get possession of the throne, but he takes great care that the blood be not spilt. For they say that it is highly improper that the blood of the great Khan be spilt upon the ground..." (Frazer, 1923, 235).

Other methods in other cultures admitted wide variations on the theme, including strangulation, drowning, being beaten with sticks, and many more. In 1688, during a palace revolution against the King of Siam, the rebellious general placed the king after his defeat in a large metal caldron and smashed his body with wooden pestles so that none of his royal blood would strike the ground.

BL⊕⊕D ⊕F +HE VAⅢPIRE

As numerous cultures struggled to define their own concepts of what blood represented to them, in Eastern Europe there seemed an overwhelming fascination with the power that lay within the blood of vampires themselves. While there were conflicting views on the topic by both church scholars and peasants alike, the blood of the vampire could be seen as either a curse or a charm depending on the region one was traveling through.

In some villages vampires were vile carriers of disease and pestilence whose very blood reeked of spiritual pollution. Before a corpse suspected of vampirism was staked, villagers often covered it with a cloth, hide, or dirt in order to avoid being splattered with its blood. Such precautions were a means of avoiding infection, which carried with it the penalty of madness, death, or vampirism if the creature's blood touched a living human.

In other communities a vampire's blood was the only real talisman against vampires. In Pomerania, on the shores of the Baltic Sea, it was believed that to ward off vampires one must dip the burial shroud in the revenant's blood and squeeze its contents into a glass of brandy before being consumed. As examined in greater detail earlier in this book, another remedy consisted of digging up the vampire while it slept during the day and smearing its blood on oneself, or, as in Russia, the blood was mixed with flour and baked into bread. Once the bread was eaten, the person was then thought to be immune from vampire attacks.

Throughout human history, blood has symbolized more than just the vague concepts of life and death, but for all intents and purposes it *was* life and death. Its presence meant that life existed and that magic and the sacred lay just under the surface of every human being. It was the most intimate part of man. If harnessed properly, it promised power, health, luck, and protection, and for some it even greased the spiritual wheels between the world of gods and mortals.

When corrupted, however, it meant death and disease and all the dark things that people feared. The traditional vampires of folklore were little more than bloated corpses or evil night spirits consumed with the desire to feed on human blood in order to maintain their own corrupted existence. It is for this reason perhaps that they were feared the most, because of their ability to invade and destroy the very life essence of humanity. As the crazed character Renfield in Bram Stoker's *Dracula* so eloquently raved, "The blood is the life! The blood is the life!"

There are more things in heaven and earth, Horatio,
Than are dreamt of in your philosophy.
　　　—WILLIAM SHAKESPEARE, *HAMLET*, ACT I, SCENE 5

10

STRANGER
THAN FICTION

Throughout the pages of this book we have searched long and hard to unravel the mysteries of the dreaded creature the world has come to know as the vampire. From the sandblown ruins of ancient Mesopotamia it was seen rising on howling desert winds as an insatiable night demon; from the sweltering jungles of the east it was heard in the pounding drums of strange cults as they called out to bloodthirsty gods; and from the mist-shrouded graveyards of Eastern Europe, villagers fled in abject terror as its shambling form moved through the tombstones on dark nights.

Over the course of this harrowing journey one important observation stands out above the rest: that the vampire has not one face but many, and the form it chooses to appear in at any given time changes depending on the needs of the culture that embraces it. In 1871 the British anthropologist Edward Burnett Tylor wrote in his definitive work *Primitive Culture* that "vampires are not mere creations of groundless fancy, but causes conceived in spiritual form to account for specific facts..." (Tylor 1994, 192).

It's true that Tylor was referring specifically to primitive notions surrounding unexplained diseases, but the same principle applies to any number of natural phenomena that early men could not account for, making vampires the ultimate explanation for that which was ultimately unexplainable.

ANCIEN+ ANSWERS

By the time vampires made their way into the cuneiform writings of the Babylonians, they were already an ancient belief among early peoples and took the forms of frightful spirits or night demons responsible for a host of evil activities. Beyond their obviously destructive traits, however, they also served to help reinforce societal norms by providing the threat of otherworldly reprisal if a taboo were broken. As examined early in this book, the *ekimmu* were evil spirits that resulted when someone died alone and without relatives to remember them or place the appropriate offerings of food and drink at their grave. According to many early societies, the worlds of the living and the dead were often closely intertwined and even impacted one another on a daily basis. If the living relative therefore did not provide sustenance for the dead, the spirits would grow famished and eventually turn to human blood to quench their hunger.

While a number of remedies existed to combat such spirits, it's telling that the most effective means was simply to perform the necessary burial rites at the grave of the one suspected of being an ekimmu and thereby uphold the conventions, so necessary for survival, that bound the individual to the familial unit.

At other times vampires acted as a sort of universal scapegoat for all the natural evils that seemed to befall people, including famines, diseases, storms, nightmares, and unexplained deaths. A host of vampiric demons existed to take the blame for these tragedies, such as the *Lamashtu, Lamme, gallu,* and *lilith.*

Of all the fiends that walked through these stories, however, it was perhaps the demoness Lilith that was most feared for her role as a child killer. Infant mortality being what it was at the time, it was easier to justify how a healthy infant had died in his or her sleep by believing that an evil force crept into the room and took the child's life. Today we call the phenomenon crib death or sudden infant death syndrome (SIDS), and even with all our medical advances we are no closer to providing an explanation to the causes of this tragedy. In instances of miscarriages or stillbirths, where spontaneous bleeding occurs, it doesn't take too much imagination to see how the demoness became associated with blood drinking as well.

DILEMMA OF THE DEAD

As the belief in vampire-like creatures moved west into Europe along the well-traveled caravan routes and migration paths, it transformed itself in order to find greater acceptance in the new lands in which it took root. Previous images of antagonistic spirits and night demons capable of shocking atrocities were replaced by a monster born from the worst of nightmares, a maniacal corpse bent on human blood. Yet despite the complete horror of this image, the revenants of Eastern Europe served an invaluable function for the communities that feared them, resolving dilemmas connected with improper burials, bodily decomposition, and the spread of highly contagious diseases.

Take, for instance, the differences between modern burial practices and those conducted as few as two hundred years ago. In the typical twenty-first century burial, when a person dies their body is first subjected to a postmortem examination by a coroner, known as an autopsy, to determine the cause and manner of death. The body then undergoes an embalming process during which the blood and other fluids are replaced with preservative chemicals to slow the rate of decomposition. After being dressed and placed in a metal coffin by a mortician, the body is lowered into a concrete vault four to six feet underground. Following a funeral service, the lid to the vault is sealed with long metal bars and the soil, originally excavated by heavy earth-moving machines, is piled back on top. By the end of the lengthy process the final remains are more secure than the national gold reserve at Fort Knox.

By contrast, burials in the past were nowhere near as efficient or as sanitary and required more of the community's limited resources and manpower. Unless the deceased was a person of nobility or wealth, most gravesites were nothing more than a shallow hole scraped from the earth with the hands and shovels of loved ones. In regions where the soil was rocky or during the winter months when the ground was frozen, the task was especially difficult. Once the grave was prepared the body was washed and dressed by family members before being wrapped in a burial shroud. Coffins were of course a luxury and few could afford them, so most bodies were placed directly into the earth with dirt or sometimes rock laid over them. In some cultures the proceedings were lengthy and filled with elaborate ceremony, while in others, or in cases of murder or suicide, they were hastily conducted with little thought. During periods of deadly outbreaks, when the body count became too much to keep up with, the bodies of the victims were simply thrown into mass graves if they were buried at all.

Improper burials often led to disturbing consequences, including bodies being washed out of graves during heavy rains or attracting hungry dogs and wolves looking for a snack. Villagers passing by were commonly treated to the horrific sights of graves in disarray with headstones toppled over, half-eaten body parts here and there, and burial sites that had been clawed at as if something were trying to dig its way out.

Many of these signs came to be interpreted as evidence that evil was afoot and that a foul vampire had taken up residence among the corpses. Even when the traditional test of having a horse wander through a cemetery until it found a grave it would not cross was used, it's easy to understand—considering that the half-exposed body smelled, the ground underfoot was unstable, and the beast could probably sense the fear of the crowd gathering around it—what the result would be.

Once a corpse was suspected of being a blood drinker, it was only a matter of time before it was disinterred and searched for signs of vampirism. Many who were unfamiliar with the way that the body breaks down often misinter-preted the natural process of decomposition for something far more sinister. For most rural communities the post-death process was a simple one: when you died, if you were a good and faithful Christian you were buried in consecrated ground where in time your body stiffened, your hair fell out, your flesh became bones and dust, your clothing rotted away, and your soul went to heaven. In cases of reported vampire out-breaks, eyewitnesses attested that the bodies of the vampires remained preserved in an unnatural state that by all descrip-tions bordered on the demonic. The face was characterized as dark or ruddy-complexioned with fresh blood around the nose and mouth; and the body, flexible and swollen to the point of bursting, was stretched as tight as a drum from all the blood it had recently engorged itself with.

A careful examination of how the human body truly de-composes after death, however, sheds light on how some of these startling observations were made by witnesses. When the body's heart ceases to pump blood through the circulatory system, gravity pulls the fluid to the lowest parts of the body. If as in many cases the corpse was buried facing downwards to prevent it from digging its way out, the blood pooled in the face, giving it a reddish appearance as the eyes protruded and the lips peeled back in a macabre sort of snarl. While rigor mortis does indeed set in initially, causing the limbs and joints to stiffen when depleted of enzymes, the condition is only temporary, and after approximately thirty-six hours the muscle fibers deteriorate, leaving the corpse as pliable as it was in life. Bacteria within the body, known as *bacillus aerogenes*, then begin to multiply, feeding on the internal organs and releasing a gangrenous gas that swells the body.

As this pressure builds, the body moves and shifts as the gas occasionally redistributes itself and blood and other fluids are forced out of the body's orifices including the eyes, mouth, and nose. Later, when would-be vampire hunters attempted to drive a stake through the chest cavity of the corpse, they were often frightened by the body giving off an eerie moan, which although they attributed it to the vampire, was actually gas forced past the undecayed vocal cords by the force of the blow. It's interesting to note that many of the early methods of dispatching vampires coincidentally inhibited the development of *bacillus aerogenes* and therefore seemed to have their desired results. Garlic, for instance, is an antiseptic that kills gangrene, while heat and sunlight impede bacterial growth.

Although many mistakenly thought that the vampire's body failed to decompose because it sustained itself with the blood of its victims, modern science reveals that there are a number of factors that affect the decomposition rate of the human body, including temperature, humidity, oxygen levels, chemical composition of the soil, and burial depth. While a body exposed to the elements can decompose in a matter of months, below the surface in a cold, airless environment free of scavengers and insects the process slows considerably. In arid regions, newly buried corpses can mummify, while in moist climates the opposite is true and saponification may develop, encasing the body in a waxy substance that also preserves the flesh.

The Benedictine monk and early vampirologist Augustin Calmet believed that certain compositions of soil aided or retarded the rate of decomposition, pointing to a crypt in a church in Toulouse, France, that housed an order of monks.

Along one wall, he wrote, the bodies remained perfectly preserved for nearly two centuries, while on the opposite wall newly interred monks decayed after only a few days. A modern example of note was discovered in the peat bogs of Denmark in the 1950s near the small village of Tollund, when workers stumbled upon the preserved body of a man from the fourth century BCE. Because of the highly acidic nature of the cold bogs and the lack of oxygen, the flesh of the "Tollund Man," as he is called, turned black and mummified. Since that time, hundreds of bog bodies have been discovered across Northern Europe in the same well-preserved condition.

One of the more feared aspects of the European vampire, however, was not their insatiable craving for human blood but that they were carriers of deadly diseases such as the bubonic plague, yellow fever, and tuberculosis. In fact, a careful study of purported vampire attacks across Europe in the sixteenth, seventeenth, and eighteenth centuries reveals that they often coincided with outbreaks of infectious epidemics. When a healthy man suddenly took to his bed with a mysterious illness and died, followed shortly thereafter by his wife, sons, and then close friends who visited him on his sickbed, it wasn't the work of microscopic bacteria inadvertently passed from one host to another, it was the presence of the vampire. In 1922 when director F. W. Murnau titled his cult classic *Nosferatu*, he chose a name that meant not "the undead" or "the blood drinker," but "plague carrier," because it came closer to the original concept of the traditional vampire in Germany.

In the folklore of Europe, vampirism itself was a communicable disease passed from the infected corpse of the revenant to that of its living victim either when it fed or when someone came into contact with its tainted blood. It's interesting to note when rifling through the eyewitness accounts of vampire attacks that the victims suffered symptoms often found in many life-threatening diseases, including:

- Failing strength or lethargy
- Symptoms that worsened at night
- Weight loss
- Feelings of heaviness in the chest
- Pale skin
- Loss of appetite
- Coughing fits that produced blood in the mucus

Even in parts of rural New England during the eighteenth and nineteenth centuries, the wasting disease now called tuberculosis was commonly thought to be the result of attacks from a family member who had become a vampire. An airborne pathogen called *Mycobacterium tuberculosis* causes tuberculosis, which usually attacks the lungs and without proper treatment kills over half of its victims. The symptoms of tuberculosis include fever, weight loss, chronic coughing, and blood-tinged mucus.

The 1892 case of a young girl named Mercy Lea Brown is one of the last known times in America that a person was exhumed due to fears of vampirism. The Brown family was living in Exeter, Rhode Island, at the time when the "bloody cough" hit, first killing Mercy's mother and then Mercy's sister Olive shortly thereafter. Sometime later, Mercy's older brother Edwin became ill also, and he and his wife moved to Colorado to seek treatment at a sanatorium famed for its healing mineral springs. While they were away, Mercy grew sick as well and died at the age of nineteen.

Edwin returned home, but his condition only worsened and neighbors began to suggest that one of the Brown family members had become a vampire after death and was now responsible for the mysterious wasting disease afflicting the family. If George Brown, the patriarch of the family, wanted to save what was left of his family, they warned, he needed to exhume the bodies and examine them for signs of vampirism.

George Brown was horrified by the notion of desecrating their graves but eventually gave in to pressure from the community. Accompanied by the local medical examiner, Dr. Harold Metcalf, Brown disinterred his wife and two daughters. First he exhumed his wife, whose remains were little more than bones and a bit of hair; then his daughter Olive, who while mummified appeared to have no blood left in her body; and finally he dug up young Mercy, who despite having been in the ground three months appeared fresh and with a rosy blush to her cheeks.

Although the doctor cautioned that it was merely a natural part of death's process, George nonetheless ordered her heart removed for further inspection. After finding thick, dark blood still in the heart, witnesses claimed that it was a sign of vampirism, and the organ was burned to ashes on a nearby rock. Afterwards, the ashes were mixed with various medicines and fed to Edwin in the hopes of breaking the vampire's curse, but, alas, he died soon after anyway.

WEIRD SCIENCE

While it's often easy to look back on the beliefs of our forebears and shake our heads in disbelief at the credulousness of their superstitions, in our own time theories surrounding the origin of the vampire continue, with speculations as colorful as anything that came before. Probably one of the most often repeated theories on the genesis of the European vampire is the idea that it stems from the unusual appearance of those suffering from the blood disease porphyria. Also known as King George III's disease, the genetic disorder causes an abnormality in the hemoglobin, sending part of the blood's pigment to the urine rather than the body's cells. Toxic levels accumulate quickly, producing a wide range of symptoms including a reddening of the eyes, skin, and teeth as well as sensitivity to sunlight and necrosis of the skin. Treatment of the disorder involves injections of heme and reducing blood volume to control iron levels.

The theory was first espoused in 1964 by Dr. Lee Illis of Guy's Hospital in London in a paper for the *Proceedings of the Royal Society of Medicine* entitled "On Porphyria and the Aetiology of Werewolves," and then again by author Nancy Garden in her 1973 book, *Vampires*. It didn't become popular, however, until it was reintroduced to the public during a lecture for the American Association for the Advancement of Science in 1985 by Canadian biochemist David Dolphin with his paper "Porphyria, Vampires, and Werewolves: The Aetiology of European Metamorphosis Legends."

Dolphin's ideas were widely accepted in large part because of the vampire boom in books and movies sweeping the Western Hemisphere and the growing trend among writers and moviemakers to modernize the creature by adding a bit of science to the mix and casting vampirism as a disease. Unfortunately for those suffering from the disorder and who now had to face the added stigma of this new label, Dolphin's knowledge was limited to that of Hollywood vampires, and none of the corpses accused of vampirism in historical texts actually displayed the characteristic of someone with porphyria.

Other theories followed this growing trend, including one proposed by the Spanish neurologist Juan Gomez-Alonso in 1998, published in the journal *Neurology*, that held that the belief in the European vampire was the result of major epidemics of rabies across Europe in the 1700s. The idea for this new theory came to Dr. Gomez-Alonso late one night as he watched the movie *Dracula* and suddenly noticed striking similarities between the vampire and victims of rabies. While researching the matter further, he uncovered a wealth of interesting correlations—including the fact that victims suffering from rabies often have the tendency to bite others and that most of the famous vampire outbreaks in Eastern Europe coincided with rabies epidemics in dogs and wolves, especially in Hungary between 1721 and 1728.

Rabies is a viral disease causing swelling in the brain and is passed through the bite of an infected animal, most commonly dogs, wolves, and bats (animals associated with vampires). Symptoms include anxiety, confusion, agitation, paranoia, hallucinations, hydrophobia, and finally death. Interestingly enough, many of the folkloric aversions attributed to vampires are also found in rabies victims. As Dr. Gomez-Alonso pointed out, "Men with rabies... react to stimuli such as water, light, odors, or mirrors with spasms of the facial and vocal muscles that can cause hoarse sounds, bared teeth, and frothing at the mouth of bloody fluid." In the past, he continued, "a man was not considered rabid if he was able to stand the sight of his own image in a mirror" (Jenkins 2010, 15–16). The deadly bite of the vampire, which could infect a victim, has its obvious parallels with rabies.

Others have surmised that victims of reported nocturnal vampire attacks also show a marked similarity to a condition known as sleep paralysis, which occurs either just before falling asleep or just upon waking, when a person finds himself or herself fully awake yet unable to move. The paralysis can last anywhere from a few seconds to a few minutes and is thought to be the result of a temporary disconnect between the brain and the body as the person drifts in and out of REM sleep. This often terrifying condition may afflict both normal sleepers and those diagnosed with disorders such as narcolepsy, cataplexy, and during the presence of hypnagogic hallucinations.

Normally those with sleep paralysis awake unable to move, with what they perceive as the sound of someone or something approaching them. Strange forms or even smells manifest along with the feeling that an immense weight is crushing the person's chest. In a few moments the paralysis wears off, and they come fully awake to find that they are completely exhausted as if they had not slept at all. In early European folklore many believed that at night an old hag or witch could leave her physical body and sit upon the chest of a sleeping victim, causing nightmares or even crushing the victim to death. In fact, the original name for the phenomenon was itself *nightmare*, from the combination of the word *night* and the Old English term *maere*, meaning "demon" or "incubus."

Perhaps the newest take on the old myth is the belief that vampires originated from individuals suffering from what psychiatrists today call *clinical vampirism*. It is also known as *Renfield's syndrome*, a term first coined by psychologist Richard Noll in his book *Bizarre Diseases of the Mind*, which compared the traits of the disorder to those exhibited by the fictional character Renfield in Bram Stoker's *Dracula*, who eats spiders and flies in order to consume their life force. Those diagnosed with this syndrome display a strong obsession for drinking blood and may develop delusions of being a vampire. The act of drinking blood carries with it an intense sexual aspect coupled with the belief that it will convey certain supernatural powers.

The condition usually occurs in males just before they reach the age of puberty when some trauma or event psychically links blood and sexuality together for them, which in turn leads to vampiric fantasies and auto-vampirism (drinking one's own blood). In more extreme examples, such as in the case of convicted serial killer Richard Trenton Chase, whose blood-drinking crimes we examined earlier, it can also intensify into necrophilia, necrophagia, cannibalism, and sadism.

The search for the truth about vampires has been a long and arduous journey through a vast collection of exotic countries, belief systems, and languages. When we first began the hunt we were standing next to an empty grave in a deserted island monastery pondering the mystery of one of history's most notorious blood drinkers, the fifteenth-century Wallachian prince Vlad Dracula Tepes. Through it all we've seen what the vampire meant to each of the cultures we examined, studying its various forms, habits, and how some mortals even took arms against it in a centuries-old struggle of good versus evil.

Yet in the end what matters most is what the vampire means to us here and now in the new age dawning before us. Is it still the thing lurking just beyond the glow of the campfire somewhere out there in the darkness, or is it ultimately the darkness that we find lurking within ourselves? Whether or not you believe in vampires, or in what form you believe they exist, will in the end come to depend on what your answer is to that very question.

In light of where we have traveled and the horrors we have seen, it is important to include a cautionary tale about the dangers of hunting vampires. On July 16, 1996, a young reporter for the New York *Village Voice* named Susan Walsh dropped her son off at her ex-husband's apartment, saying she would be running some quick errands. At the time, Susan was investigating the vampire clubs then springing up in Greenwich Village, as well as sinister reports of kidnappings and murders connected to the modern blood drinkers.

In her search for the truth some believe she may have delved too far by immersing herself in the vampyre subculture and dating a man who believed he was a vampire. That day she told her ex-husband that she would be back in a few minutes, but she was never seen again. A subsequent search of her apartment revealed that she had taken none of her personal belongings nor her pager or wallet. Some say she committed suicide or ran afoul of the Russian mafia, but others claim that she became a victim of the very vampires she was hunting. Regardless of which version you choose to believe, Susan Walsh dropped off the face of the earth, and her case remains open and unsolved to this day.

Today the monastery at Lake Snagov has become something of a tourist shrine for vampire fans the world over, who make pilgrimages to the site to snap photos of the empty grave and leave flowers or other items. Up until World War II the archeological evidence collected from the second grave was housed in the city of Bucharest's History Museum, at which time it was transferred by convicts to the mountains near Valenii de Munte in southern Romania (coincidentally Dracula's former homeland) for safekeeping.

During transport the artifacts thought to belong to Dracula disappeared, removing any hope of solving the riddle of the empty grave and ensuring for generations to come that the hunt for the truth about Dracula and the legend of the vampire will go on.

BIBLI⊕GRAPHY

Barber, Paul. *Vampires, Burial, and Death: Folklore and Reality.* New Haven, CT: Yale University Press, 1988.

Bartlett, W. B., and Flavia Idriceanu. *Legends of Blood: The Vampire in History and Myth.* Westport, CT: Praeger, 2006.

Bataille, Georges. *The Trial of Gilles de Rais.* Translated by Richard Robinson. Los Angeles: Amok, 1991. (Originally published in French in 1965.)

Belanger, Michelle A. *The Psychic Vampire Codex: A Manual of Magick and Energy Work.* Boston: Weiser Books, 2004.

The Bhagavad Gita. Translated by W. J. Johnson. Oxford: Oxford University Press, 2004.

Blackstone, William, John Hovenden, and Archer Ryland. *Commentaries on the Laws of England in Four Books, 19th edition.* London: S. Sweet, 1836.

Brown, David E. *Vampiro: The Vampire Bat in Fact and Fantasy.* Salt Lake City: University of Utah Press, 1999.

Byron, George Gordon Byron. *Byron: Poetical Works.* Edited by Frederick Page. Oxford: Oxford University Press, 1970.

Calmet, Augustin, and Gillian Bennett. *The Phantom World: Myth, Legend and Folklore.* Ware, UK: Wordsworth Editions in Association with the Folklore Society, 2001. (Originally published in 1746.)

Ciuncanu, Gigi. "O gorjeanca a infipt un cui in inima concubinului mort" (A Gorjean Stuck a Nail through the Heart of Her Dead Lover), *Ziua* (Bucharest, Romania), November 24, 1998.

Craft, Kimberly L. *Infamous Lady: The True Story of Countess Erzsébet Báthory*. Lexington, KY: Kimberly L. Craft, 2009.

Curtis, Dan, Robert Costello, Jonathan Frid, Grayson Hall, Joan Bennett, Louis Edmonds, Nancy Barrett, Dana Elcar, and John Karlen. Dan Curtis Productions. *Dark Shadows. DVD Collection 1*. Orland Park, IL: MPI Home Video, 2002.

Deane, Hamilton, John L. Bladerston, and Bram Stoker. *Dracula: The Vampire Play in Three Acts*. New York: S. French, 1960.

Dunn-Mascetti, Manuela. *Vampire: The Complete Guide to the World of the Undead*. New York: Viking Studio Books, 1992.

Florescu, Radu R., and Raymond T McNally. *Dracula, Prince of Many Faces: His Life and His Times*. Boston: Little, Brown, 1989.

Fortune, Dion. *Psychic Self-Defense*. York Beach, ME: Samuel Weiser, 2001. (Originally published in 1930 by Rider & Company, London.)

Frazer, James George. *The Golden Bough: A Study in Magic and Religion. Volume 1*. New York: Macmillan and Co., 1923.

Garden, Nancy. *Vampires*. Philadelphia: Lippincott, 1973.

Gardner, John, John Maier, and Richard A. Henshaw. *Gilgamesh: Translated from the Sîn-leqi-unninni Version*. New York: Knopf, 1984.

Goethe, Johann Wolfgang von. *The Bride of Corinth*. Translated by Charles Tomlinson. London: Nutt, 1890.

Gomez-Alonso, Juan. "Rabies: A Possible Explanation for the Vampire Legend." *Neurology*, 51:3 (September 1998), 856–59.

González-Wippler, Migene. *The Complete Book of Spells, Ceremonies & Magic*, 2nd edition. St. Paul, MN: Llewellyn Publications, 1988. (Originally published in 1978 by Crown Publishers, New York.)

Guiley, Rosemary Ellen. *The Encyclopedia of Vampires, Werewolves, and Other Monsters*. New York: Facts on File, 2005.

Hacker, Joseph, and Abraham M. Habermann. *The Alphabet of Ben Sira: Facsimile of the Constantinople 1519 Edition*. Verona, Italy: Valmadonna Trust Library, 1997.

Hanson, Victor Davis. *Carnage and Culture: Landmark Battles in the Rise of Western Power*. New York: Doubleday, 2001.

Hesiod. *Hesiod, the Homeric Hymns, and Homerica*. Translated by Hugh G. Evelyn-White. London: W. Heinemann, 1914.

Homer. *The Odyssey*. Translated by Samuel Butler. London: A. C. Fifield, 1900.

"Immigrant's Fears of Vampires Led to Death," *The Times*. (London), January 9, 1973.

Institoris, Heinrich, and Jakob Sprenger. *Malleus Maleficarum*. Edited and translated by Christopher S. Mackay. Cambridge: Cambridge University Press, 2006.

Jenkins, Mark Collins. *Vampire Forensics: Uncovering the Origins of an Enduring Legend*. Washington, DC: National Geographic, 2010.

Jones, Aphrodite. *The Embrace: A True Vampire Story*. New York: Pocket Books, 1999.

Karg, Barbara, Arjean Spaite, and Rick Sutherland. *The Everything Vampire Book: From Vlad the Impaler to the Vampire Lestat—A History of Vampires in Literature, Film, and Legend*. Avon, MA: Adams Media, 2009.

Karma-glin-pa, Francesca Fremantle, and Chögyam Trungpa. *The Tibetan Book of the Dead: The Great Liberation through Hearing in the Bardo*. Berkeley, CA: Shambhala, 1975.

Konstantinos. *Vampires: The Occult Truth*. St. Paul, MN: Llewellyn Publications, 1996.

Laycock, Joseph. *Vampires Today: The Truth about Modern Vampirism*. Westport, CT: Praeger, 2009.

Le Fanu, Joseph Sheridan, and Robert Tracy. *In a Glass Darkly*. (The World's Classics.) Oxford: Oxford University Press, 1993.

Leeming, David A. *Creation Myths of the World: An Encyclopedia*. Santa Barbara, CA: ABC-CLIO, 2010.

Malham, John and William Oldys, eds. *The Harleian Miscellany: Or, a Collection of Scarce, Curious, and Entertaining Pamphlets and Tracts, as Well in Manuscript as in Print, Found in the Late Earl of Oxford's Library, Interspersed with Historical, Political, and Critical Notes, Vol. XI*. London: Printed for R. Dutton, 1808–11.

More, Henry. *An Antidote Against Atheism, or, An Appeal to the Natural Faculties of the Minde of Man*. Bristol, UK: Thoemmes Press, 1997. (Originally published in 1653.)

Murnau, F. W., Henrik Galeen, Max Schreck, Gustav von Wangenheim, Alexander Granach, Greta Schroeder-Matrey, and Bram Stoker. *Nosferatu: A Symphony of Horror*. Blackhawk Films Collection. Chatsworth, CA: Image Entertainment, 2000.

Noll, Richard. *Bizarre Diseases of the Mind*. New York: Berkley Books, 1990.

O'Donnell, Elliott. *Strange Cults and Secret Societies of Modern London*. New York: E. P. Dutton & Co., 1935.

Philostratus. *The Life of Appollonius of Tyana: The Epistles of Appollonius and the Treatise of Eusebius, Vol. 1*. (Loeb Classical Library Series.) Translated by F. C. Conybeare. London: Heinemann, 1950. Translation first published in 1912.

Polidori, John William. *The Vampyre and Other Writings*. Edited by Franklin Charles Bishop. Manchester, UK: Carcanet, 2005.

Ralston, William Ralston Shedden. *The Songs of the Russian People*. London: Ellis & Green, 1872.

Ramsland, Katherine M. *The Forensic Psychology of Criminal Minds*. New York: Berkley Boulevard, 2010.

———. *The Science of Vampires*. New York: Berkley Boulevard, 2002.

Reid, Patrick V., ed. *Readings in Western Religious Thought: The Ancient World*. New York: Paulist Press, 1987.

Rice, Anne. *Interview with the Vampire: A Novel*. New York: Knopf, 1976.

Robertson, John. "Man with Vampire Fantasy Killed Friend to Drink Blood, Court Told," *The Scotsman* (Edinburgh, Scotland), September 30, 2003.

Rowlatt, Justin. "Vampire Couple Jailed for Satanic Murder," *The Independent* (London), February 1, 2002.

Rymer, James Malcolm, and Thomas Peckett Prest. *Varney, the Vampire: or, The Feast of Blood*. Crestline, CA: Zittaw Press, 2007. (Originally published in 1847.)

Scoffern, John. *Stray Leaves of Science and Folk-lore*. London: Tinsley Bros., 1870.

Southey, Robert. *Thalaba the Destroyer: 1801*. (Revolution and Romanticism, 1789–1834 series.) Oxford: Woodstock Books, 1991. (Originally published in 1801.)

Stoker, Bram. *Dracula*. London: Penguin, 2003. (Originally published in 1897.)

Summers, Montague. *The Vampire in Europe*. Whitefish, MT: Kessinger Publications, 2003.

———. *The Vampire in Lore and Legend*. Mineola, NY: Dover Publications, 2001.

———. *Vampires and Vampirism*. Mineola, NY: Dover Publications, 2005.

Thompson, Reginald Campbell, trans. *The Devils and Evil Spirits of Babylonia, Being Babylonian and Assyrian Incantations against the Demons ... and Kindred Evil Spirits, Which Attack Mankind*. (Luzac's Semitic Text and Translation series.) London: Luzac and Co., 1903.

———. *Semitic Magic: Its Origins and Development*. (Luzac's Oriental Religious series, vol. 3.) London: Luzac and Co., 1908.

Tylor, Edward Burnett. *Primitive Culture: Researches into the Development of Mythology, Philosophy, Religion, Art, and Custom*. (The Collected Works of Edward Burnett Tylor, vol.

2.) London: Routledge/Thoemmes, 1994. (Originally published in 1871.)

Voltaire (François-Marie Arouet). *A Philosophical Dictionary: From the French of M. de Voltaire with Additional Notes, Both Critical and Argumentative, Part 2.* Boston: J. P. Mendum, 1856.

William, of Newburgh, P. G. Walsh, and M. J. Kennedy. *The History of English Affairs.* (Aris & Phillips Classical Texts.) Warminster, UK: Aris & Phillips, 1988.

Wright, Dudley. *The Book of Vampires.* New York: Dorset Press, 1987.

TO WRITE TO THE AUTHOR

If you wish to contact the author or would like more information about this book, please write to the author in care of Llewellyn Worldwide Ltd. and we will forward your request. Both the author and publisher appreciate hearing from you and learning of your enjoyment of this book and how it has helped you. Llewellyn Worldwide Ltd. cannot guarantee that every letter written to the author can be answered, but all will be forwarded. Please write to:

Brian Righi
℅ Llewellyn Worldwide
2143 Wooddale Drive
Woodbury, MN 55125-2989

Please enclose a self-addressed stamped envelope for reply, or $1.00 to cover costs. If outside the USA, enclose an international postal reply coupon.

GET MORE AT **LLEWELLYN.COM**

Visit us online to browse hundreds of our books and decks, plus sign up to receive our e-newsletters and exclusive online offers.

- **Free tarot readings • Spell-a-Day • Moon phases**
- **Recipes, spells, and tips • Blogs • Encyclopedia**
- **Author interviews, articles, and upcoming events**

GET SOCIAL WITH **LLEWELLYN**

Find us on Facebook
www.Facebook.com/LlewellynBooks

Follow us on

twitter™
www.Twitter.com/Llewellynbooks

GET BOOKS AT **LLEWELLYN**

LLEWELLYN ORDERING INFORMATION

Order online: Visit our website at www.llewellyn.com to select your books and place an order on our secure server.

Order by phone:
- Call toll free within the U.S. at 1-877-NEW-WRLD (1-877-639-9753)
- Call toll free within Canada at 1-866-NEW-WRLD (1-866-639-9753)
- We accept VISA, MasterCard, and American Express

Order by mail:
Send the full price of your order (MN residents add 6.875% sales tax) in U.S. funds, plus postage and handling to: Llewellyn Worldwide, 2143 Wooddale Drive Woodbury, MN 55125-2989

POSTAGE AND HANDLING:

STANDARD: (U.S. & Canada)
(Please allow 12 business days)
$25.00 and under, add $4.00.
$25.01 and over, FREE SHIPPING.

INTERNATIONAL ORDERS (airmail only):
$16.00 for one book, plus $3.00 for each additional book.

Visit us online for more shipping options. Prices subject to change.

FREE CATALOG!

To order, call
1-877-NEW-WRLD
ext. 8236
or visit our website

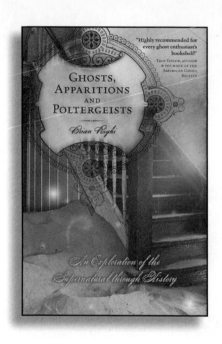

GHOSTS, APPARITIONS AND POLTERGEISTS

Brian Righi

*An Exploration of the
Supernatural through History*

Ghosts, Apparitions and Poltergeists
An Exploration of the Supernatural through History
BRIAN RIGHI

As the perfect manual for the ghost enthusiast, aspiring ghost hunter, or anyone who likes spine-tingling true tales, this book has something for everyone! Paranormal investigator Brian Righi examines the stories behind famous ghosts through history, ghost hunting and the original ghostbusters, mediums, spirit communication, spirits, apparitions, poltergeists, and more.

This unique ghoulish guide blends the history of the paranormal and paranormal investigations (including some infamous cases) with the ghost stories that accompany them. It can be read as either a handbook for ghost hunters or as a collection of true scary tales for pure enjoyment.

From ancient Babylon to nineteenth-century séance chambers to modern-day ghost hunts, Righi will take you on a fascinating exploration of the supernatural. You will venture into creepy moonlit cemeteries, ghost ships, and haunted castles; learn how to conduct a ghost hunt of your own; and spend time with some of the greatest ghost hunters ever to walk through a haunted house.

978-0-7387-1363-2, 240 pp., 5³⁄₁₆ x 8   **$15.95**

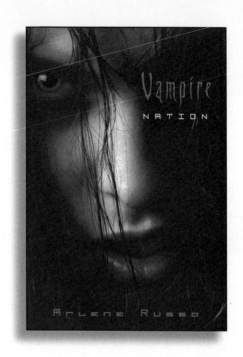

Vampire Nation

ARLENE RUSSO

Do vampires exist among us? Of course! From the revelation that Robin Hood was a vampire to the shocking evidence that Prince Charles is a descendant of Vlad the Impaler, this book exposes the truth about vampires like never before.

Available in the U.S. after taking the United Kingdom by storm, *Vampire Nation* brings you into the heart of vampire culture as vampire expert Russo reveals vampires' strange rituals and intriguing practices. Unearth centuries-old folklore, superstitions, and myths—such as the belief that vampires fear sunlight. Dozens of actual vampires offer their chilling true accounts and real-life stories. Get an insider's look at how vampires awaken to their nature, how they find and feed on human blood and psychic energy, where they live, and many other bloodcurdling facts.

Shrouded in secrecy no more, this revelatory book dares you to enter the little known and fascinating underground world of vampires.

978-0-7387-1456-1, 240 pp., 6 x 9   **$15.95**

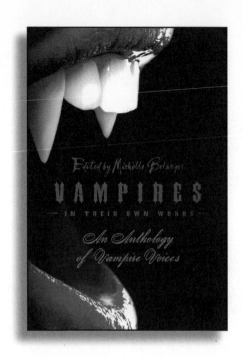

Edited by Michelle Belanger

VAMPIRES
— IN THEIR OWN WORDS —
An Anthology of Vampire Voices

Vampires in Their Own Words

An Anthology of Vampire Voices

EDITED BY MICHELLE BELANGER

Michelle Belanger, an expert on vampirism and a self-professed psychic vampire, accomplishes a feat no one has ever managed before. She's convinced nearly two dozen real-life vampires to break the code of silence that has kept this fascinating community shrouded in secrecy . . . until now.

This diverse collection of contributors—including Raven Kaldera, Madame X, and Sanguinarius—speak candidly about their beliefs, practices, and how they awakened to their identities as vampires. You'll hear firsthand from psychic vampires who feed on energy for spiritual and physical nourishment and from sanguine vampires who drink actual blood. These true stories describe the compulsion to feed and what it feels like, working with donors, living with a social stigma, ethical principles, and other unique aspects of this underground culture.

978-0-7387-1220-8, 288 pp., 6 x 9   **$15.95**

PSYCHIC VAMPIRES

PROTECTION FROM ENERGY PREDATORS & PARASITES

JOE SLATE PH.D.

Psychic Vampires
Protection from Energy Predators & Parasites
JOE H. SLATE, PH.D.

Is somebody sucking your life-force energy?

Consuming energy instead of blood, psychic vampires come in a variety of unsuspecting guises. In this unique approach to the subject, you will be introduced to a trio of new thieves: (1) group vampires, organized efforts of predator corporations and institutions; (2) parasitic vampires, an inner vampire state that feeds on your internal energy resources; and (3) global vampirism, widespread conditions that erode the human potential for growth and progress.

Exploring environmental, developmental, and past-life factors, *Psychic Vampires* incorporates practical, step-by-step empowerment procedures that everyone can use to protect themselves and replenish their own energy reserves.

978-0-7387-0191-2, 264 pp., 6 x 9   **$16.95**
